The Indispensable Guide to Pastoral Care

Sharyl B. Peterson

THE
PILGRIM
PRESS
Cleveland

The Pilgrim Press
700 Prospect Avenue
Cleveland, Ohio 44115-1100
thepilgrimpress.com

♻ Printed in the United States of America on acid-free paper that contains post-consumer fiber.

17 16 15 14 13   6 5 4 3

Library of Congress Cataloging-in-Publication Data
Peterson, Sharyl B., 1951-
    The indispensable guide to pastoral care / Sharyl B. Peterson.
      p. cm.
    Includes bibliographical references.
    ISBN-13: 978-0-8298-1778-2 (alk. paper)
      1. Pastoral care. 2. Pastoral theology. I. Title.
    BV4011.3.P49 2008
    253 – dc22

                                        2007040373

Contents

In the first few centuries of the Christian church, care for others was believed to be a fundamental responsibility of every person who claimed to be a Christian. As the church became more institutionalized, the care of God's people was given over to those specially authorized by the church to provide such care — bishops and clergy. As this happened, care focused on moral conduct, or teaching people what was right and what was wrong, and encouraging them to do the right thing. This view still prevails among more conservative traditions today, and is reemerging among some more liberal traditions as well.

This approach to pastoral care lasted nearly seventeen centuries, up to the time of the Reformation. Then Roman Catholic and emerging Protestant understandings of pastoral care began to diverge, with the former continuing to center on the sacramental system, and the latter, informed by the Social Gospel movement, increasingly understanding their task as "shepherding souls" or nurturing deeper relationships with those they shepherded.

Those differences continue today, with new ones added to the mix. Within Protestantism, caregivers in evangelical traditions tend to focus more on moral guidance and correction while those from mainline traditions focus more on personal growth and unconditional love. Mainline caregivers are also more likely to integrate into their pastoral practice new knowledge from the behavioral and medical sciences, such as the importance of social location.[9]

Summary

Like your forefathers and foremothers in faith, you have been blessed by God. So you are called to bless others by sharing God's love with them. The form of blessing that you offer through the care called "pastoral" has certain important features: Pastoral care embodies active love, and is grounded in relationship with God and with others. It recognizes persons' social locations and communal contexts. And it draws on a range of resources. Above all, it is your relationship with God, and that of the careseeker, and the way those are embodied in your care which make it "pastoral." You are blessed to journey with those souls whose care God has entrusted to you. And while you cannot know the journey's end, you can trust the One who journeys with you, holding, strengthening, and encouraging you as you travel forward.

Notes

1. Alastair Campbell, in *Integrity of Pastoral Care*, ed. David Lyall (Trowbridge: Cromwell Press, 2001), 6, writes: "Pastoral care is surprisingly simple. It has one fundamental aim: to help people know love, both as something to be received and as something to give. The summary of Jesus of all the Law and the Prophets in the two great (Old Testament) texts on love tells us . . . all we need to know about the tasks of Ministry."

2. John Quinlan, *Pastoral Relatedness: The Essence of Pastoral Care* (Lanham, MD: University Press of America, 2002), 18–19.

3. For ease of use, I will typically use the term "careseeker" (and sometimes "care-receiver") throughout to refer to persons to whom pastors offer care. They may include parishioners, hospital patients, spiritual directees, or others.

4. G. H. Tucker, "Old Testament and Apocrypha, Traditions, and Theology of Care In," *Dictionary of Pastoral Care and Counseling*, ed. Rodney J. Hunter (Nashville: Abingdon Press, 1990), 799.

5. Nancy J. Ramsay, ed., *Pastoral Care and Counseling: Redefining the Paradigms* (Nashville: Abingdon Press, 2004), 1–2; there is greater focus on this topic in the chapters "Pastoral Theology as Public Theology" by Bonnie J. Miller-McLemore, and "Methods in Pastoral Theology, Care, and Counseling" by Joretta L. Marshall.

6. A very important new theory of behavior that takes all of this into account and is especially helpful for pastoral caregivers from all traditions is called "family systems theory." See Resources, page 131 below.

7. Quinlan, *Pastoral Relatedness*, 25.

8. All names used in the illustrations are fictitious, and some details have been changed to preserve confidentiality.

9. If you are likely to be offering pastoral care in a setting where many care-receivers come from traditions other than your own (for example, as a hospital chaplain), it would be very useful for you to understand these issues well.

Chapter Two

Being in Right Relationship

*God longs for us to be in right relationship with each other. . . . In
God's vision for creation, people relate to each other in particular
ways. These relationships are characterized by honor, respect,
love, and care. Right relationships are creative, mutual, and
generative: life-giving things are birthed. When we are in right
relationship we embody these God-intended ways of being with
each other.*[1]

BEING IN "right relationship" is at the core of what we mean
when we talk about ethics in pastoral care. It has to do with
treating those for whom you care in ways that are compassionate, just, and humane; ways that embody integrity, mutuality,
and equality; ways that recognize and honor all persons' worth
as beloved children of God.

Ethical principles are those principles of love, justice, honor, respect, and care that guide us in our work, helping us discern the
things we ought to do and ought not to do in order to nourish and
sustain right relationship between ourselves, our communities,
and those we serve.

What Principles Shall We Choose?

Each profession has its own set of guiding ethical principles. My
first professional training, before I entered ministry, was in the
field of psychology. Its guiding body, the American Psychological Association (APA), has a lengthy list of principles to which

psychologists agree to adhere as they do their work, whether as professors, researchers, or therapists.

While many professional associations like the APA established rules for ethical practice long ago, churches have been slower to do so. It was long assumed that because ministers are trying to do God's work, and that most people who go into ministry are well-intentioned, honest, and good, churches didn't have to worry about developing such guidelines to regulate ministers' conduct.

Those assumptions were wrong. While most ministers are indeed good people, they are also fallible human beings who sometimes do very wrong things. For various reasons, clergy may provide services for which they do not have appropriate training or expertise, and end up harming those they serve. Sexual misconduct by clergy has become a serious concern for every denomination. Public awareness of domestic violence and child and elder abuse has increased, raising new ethical questions about appropriate responsibilities and limits for clergy in such situations. Most mainline denominations and many individual churches have now developed their own sets of ethical guidelines to which it is hoped their ministers will adhere.

The goal is to try to ensure that careseekers are respected and honored in their personhood, treated appropriately, and assured of personal safety when they receive pastoral care. So, familiarize yourself with the ethical guidelines of your denomination or faith body. They will help you understand and respond to issues like those below.

Helen's Great-Grandson

Imagine you are sitting in your office one afternoon when a woman knocks on the door and asks if you have a minute to talk. Helen is a parishioner whom you don't know very well. You guess she is in her late seventies, are pretty sure she is married, and know she serves faithfully on the Altar Guild.

She is clearly distressed, begins to weep, and blurts out: "It's my great-grandson. I think his foster dad is hurting him. I don't know if his mom — my granddaughter — knows or not. I don't know what to do. I thought maybe you could do something, since you're a minister. Oh, and my husband doesn't know I'm here. He's my second husband, so he's not really related to my granddaughter, but he really believes in family privacy, and if he knew I was telling anyone about this, he'd kill me. You can't let him or anyone else know that I talked to you about this."

Before reading on, stop for a minute and think about this situation. What ethical issues or questions occur to you? Make some notes for yourself before reading further.

Your list may include:

♦ *Confidentiality*: Helen has asked you not to let her husband or anybody else know you've had this conversation. Can you maintain confidentiality if someone is at risk? If you need help deciding what to do here, is there anyone you can ethically tell about this?

♦ *Safety of child*: What does Helen mean by the foster father "hurting" her great-grandson? Is it abuse? Depending on the great-grandson's age and which state you live in, you may be required to report suspected abuse, whether or not you know for a fact that it is occurring.

♦ *Safety of reporter*: Is Helen truly at risk if her husband finds out she has discussed this situation with you?

♦ *Your expertise*: What can you reasonably offer Helen by way of a caring response, and what can you not do? How do your commitments to her relate to your commitments to the great-grandson, to the husband, and to the wider community that holds you accountable? What community resources might help meet some of her needs?

What may have seemed a simple caregiving situation is in fact filled with ethical complexities about which we need to be aware, both pastorally and legally.

Key Ethical Principles

Confidentiality

What a careseeker tells a caregiver may not be shared with anyone else without the careseeker's explicit permission to share it.[2] It's that simple.

Confidentiality is essential in pastoral care relationships because it provides the foundation for building trust. Much of what careseekers share with you — whether worrisome medical news, anger about a broken relationship, uncertainty about an important decision, or something else — is not information they want shared with others until they are ready to share it themselves. So a person who confides something to you needs to be able to trust that you will not tell it to others, including other parishioners, your family members, or someone significant in the careseeker's life.

While most of us understand that confidentiality is important, it is not always easy to maintain. Imagine that Bill complains to you that Linda, who chairs the church committee on which Bill serves, is not doing her committee work responsibly. You'd like to be able to ask Bill to grant Linda a little grace, because you know she is struggling through a painful divorce. However, that information is confidential, so you can't make the request. Or imagine you have been dealing with a very distressing situation with a hospital patient, and you go home exhausted. You'd like to be able to tell your spouse what you've been going through and why you are so tired, but the information is confidential, and it is not okay to share what happened.

Many circumstances occur where you will be tempted to share something you have learned in confidence. Yet to minister effectively, you cannot do so except under certain circumstances described below. If you want careseekers to trust you — which is crucial if you are to help them — they must know that what they tell you will stay between the two of you unless they grant you permission to share it with someone else.

How does this apply in Helen's situation? She has made it clear that what she is telling you is not to be shared with anyone else. The basic rule of confidentiality means you cannot share her concerns with her husband, granddaughter, or anyone else. And you must follow that rule unless the great-grandson is a minor, in which case special considerations apply.

Required Reporting

In the past two decades, we have become much more aware of the staggeringly high incidence of child neglect and child abuse. In response, every state has passed laws attempting to protect children from such maltreatment. An increasing number of states have also passed laws attempting to protect other at-risk groups of people, including elders, from abuse or mistreatment.

Such laws include identifying which people — called "mandatory reporters" — are required to report suspected child (or elder) abuse or neglect. Every state requires that any "professional who works with children" report reasonable suspicions of maltreatment. In addition, twenty-five states specifically list clergy as mandated reporters. Many other states include them in the "any person" category, where "any person" (not just those working in particular settings or professions) who has reason to suspect abuse or neglect is required to report it to the appropriate agency. To learn the specific laws in your state, check the Internet or your local Child and Adult Protection office.

If you have reason to suspect that a child or elder is being abused, concern for the victim's well-being supersedes laws of confidentiality. Contact the appropriate agency and report the suspected abuse. If you are working in a church setting, that will probably mean a call to the local County Child or Adult Protective Services (or Child or Elders Welfare Department). If you work in an institutional setting (for example, a hospital, college or university, or group home), you will usually first contact the appropriate person in your institution, and may then also need to contact the appropriate governmental office.

In our example, this means you need to find out first what Helen meant by the foster father "hurting" her great-grandson. If it appears to be any form of abuse or neglect, you need to find out how old the great-grandson is. If he is a minor, you must contact the appropriate authorities. If in doubt, make the contact anyway, and professionals with more experience than yourself can help you determine whether or not the situation needs to be reported and followed up on.

Safety

A second set of circumstances that may cause you to violate confidentiality is when the safety of the careseeker, or of someone toward whom they express harmful intentions, appears to be at serious risk.

It is fairly common for parishioners who are struggling with hard things to wonder aloud whether they might not "be better off dead," and for local church pastors to receive telephone calls from people (often not parishioners) who are in despair, and thinking of ending their lives. In either case, you need to *immediately* seek additional support for the person. Even if they have asked you to keep in confidence what they have told you, this is a situation where the information must be shared for their greater good.

It is much less common, but not unheard of, for a careseeker to tell the caregiver that he or she is thinking about harming someone else. For example, a man we'll call "Steve" had met with his pastor several times to talk about his anger at the amount of time and energy his wife was spending on her career. When she called to say that she would be home late because of an unexpected emergency at work, Steve called the church, and said to his pastor with rage resonating in his voice, "I've just about had enough. Maybe I'll just shoot her so we don't have to keep going through this."

Even if Steve has asked you not to tell anyone else about his thoughts or intentions, if you believe his suggestion of doing harm to his wife is serious, you have two responsibilities. The first is to communicate immediately with the person under threat, in this case, the wife. She then has a choice about what actions to take to protect herself. Your second responsibility is to communicate with the appropriate governmental body, which, depending on the state, might be a law enforcement official or a local hospital. People who present a danger to themselves or to others may be arrested or placed in a mental health facility.

If you think a person is potentially suicidal, call the local suicide hotline, hospital, or sheriff's office at once. If someone threatens to harm someone else, call the sheriff's office or 911. People who have more training in this area than you do will assess the risks and recommend a course of action. Even if you have doubts about how serious the threat is, you cannot ethically take a chance with the safety of a careseeker or of someone else. Law enforcement and medical professionals would much rather you call and be wrong than not call and have a tragedy occur.

In Helen's situation, you would want to seriously assess her comment that "my husband would kill me if I tell anyone else." She may well be speaking metaphorically, but there may also be issues in their relationship that need to be attended to — at once.

Knowing Your Limits

We all have limits to our training and ability to deal with situations. No one in ministry knows everything there is to know or do.

You may become aware of your limits when a person asks you a question to which you don't know how to respond. For example, when a father's teenage son is killed in a car wreck, he may ask questions like "Why couldn't I have died instead of my child?" or "Why would God do this to me?" Or you may realize your limits when you get into a situation where a person needs care and you have no idea what to do. For example, a parishioner calls late at night to tell you that her daughter has been raped, and they need your help.

In ministry, you will find you are more gifted in some areas than others, perhaps more competent at preaching than at leading a confirmation class, or more at ease doing hospital visits than caring for the recently bereaved. We all have our limits, in gifts, training, experience, and expertise. Yet we can also push those limits once we recognize them, first, by developing new skills, and second, by learning when to make referrals.

Making Referrals

When situations arise in our ministries that demand more than we can ethically and responsibly provide, it is time to make a referral — time to connect that careseeker with a caregiver who can help them in a way that we cannot.

One of the most common referrals you will make is for people who need professional therapeutic help. If you are a good listener, it may be tempting to believe that you are able to help people with healing in the arena of mental health, such as with anxiety, addictions, unhealthy marriages, clinical depression, or other mental health disorders. However, unless you are a trained counselor, you do not have the required skills. Recognize your limitations in this area, listen, assess, know what local resources are available, and then make a referral.

Making a referral is not about your shortcomings, but about your ability to acknowledge the limits of what you know and can do, and your loving and ethical choice to help careseekers get the assistance they need.

In Helen's case, you would assess what kind of support she requires. Does she need you to make a call to an agency that she doesn't feel able to make? Do she and her husband need marriage counseling? Does she need assistance that lies outside the realm of pastoral care? After carefully listening, you can determine whether

2. Confidentiality is not the same as professional privilege. There is not room here to discuss the differences, but it is helpful to know how they are different, since, in certain circumstances, notes or records you may keep about pastoral care can be legally subpoenaed. See Resources, page 131 below.

3. Ronald H. Stein, *Ethical Issues in Counseling* (Buffalo, NY: Prometheus Books, 1990), 109.

Chapter Three

The Practice of Presence

Human presence is a creative and turbulent sacrament, a visible sign of invisible grace.[1]

THE PHONE RINGS. As you grope for the receiver, you notice it is only 4:45 a.m. A call at this hour is unlikely to be good news. You croak "hello" and hear the weeping voice of a parishioner's adult son. His mother has struggled with breast cancer for the past five years, and now, he says, she is gone. Will you come, please?

You find some clothes and grab a granola bar to eat in the car. As you drive through the predawn darkness, you pray and think, trying to ignore your own feelings of grief. There will be time for those later. Right now, your call is to go and be with these people whose hearts you know are breaking. What will you say? What will you do when you get there? How can you help? Your prayer is likely something like: "Lord, comfort them, and help me to help them through this."

The answer to your questions and your prayer involves a particular way of being present with others. In this chapter, we reflect on how that presence is embodied, developed, and nurtured.

Being There

Perhaps the greatest blessing we can offer one another is that of authentic presence, which means being as completely there with the other person as you are able. It means being focused on and attentive to them, and where they are at that moment. It involves creating a safe space for the other where the pieces of their soul can rest when they feel shattered beyond repair. It is about helping them feel the loving arms of God holding them warmly.

It is not about knowing exactly the right thing to say or do. It is not about knowing more than the other about what they need, nor about fixing them or their situation. It is about being in the moment with them, offering your healthy Self to be with their hurting Self, and together being grateful for the One who is also there with you.

This can be hard to accept because most of us caregivers want to know what we can do to help others, or what we can say to help wounded souls move to a healthier, more whole place in their lives. Yet what caregivers most need to learn is simply how to be — with and for others.

People who are hurting are yearning to feel God's presence with them, and you, as a representative of that presence, are the next best thing. As you sit with them, listen to them, and show them they are not alone, you provide a visible sign of invisible grace.

But I'm Afraid

All of us are afraid at least some of the time when we do this thing called pastoral care. We are afraid that we don't know enough, won't say the right thing, or will say the wrong thing — that just being there won't be enough, or that we will do it wrong, whatever "it" is.

Over time and with practice, you will learn that most of those fears are unfounded. True, you aren't always going to know everything you need to, and you are not always going to do it right. You will sometimes make mistakes, even after years of experience. You may say something that could have been said better, or not think in the moment to do something that might have been helpful. But no one does it right all the time, and in much of pastoral care, there is seldom a clearly defined "right" thing to do.

Good caregivers bring their imperfect selves to this work. And as we do it, over and over, we grow and learn, trusting that God calls us not to be perfect but to be faithful, and to simply and humbly offer the best care we can.

Being Aware

To be present means getting past *you* (while bringing your Self fully and completely into the situation) to *them*. It's about being real and taking risks to let yourself be known, even as you are inviting others to let themselves be known — to you, to themselves, and to God. Several factors affect this process.

Prejudices and Biases

Every person grows up in a particular context, shaped by gender, race, ethnicity, socioeconomic background, and more. One result is that we are often more comfortable with people like ourselves — and less comfortable around people who are significantly different from us in some way.

Depending on what we are taught in childhood, we may develop certain beliefs or attitudes about particular groups of people. If negative, these beliefs are called prejudices. Although mature adults may try to outgrow these attitudes, they often remain part of one's psyche, and so may show up unexpectedly in pastoral encounters. For example, you may find that another person's race or ethnicity makes it harder for you to understand them, their situation, or their needs. Or you may find yourself feeling uncomfortable or behaving awkwardly when you are working with someone of a particular socioeconomic background or educational level that is different from your own.

Be aware of this. When you find yourself having difficulty ministering to another person, ask yourself what about them may be raising your anxiety or altering your normal relational style. Then you can work on those barriers in yourself that are getting between you and your ability to minister to the other person.

Hooks (a.k.a. Transference)

You will almost certainly meet some people in your ministry whom you don't like. Some you will dislike because of the way they behave, for example, the parishioner who is invariably rude to you on Sunday mornings, or the nurse on a unit you serve as chaplain who is always critical toward co-workers and patients.

Some you will dislike not because of their behavior, but because they "hook" some issue from your life history. For example, the man who frequently stops by to complain about things you're doing wrong — and unwittingly reminds you of your own highly critical father. Or the woman who comes asking for counsel bearing bruises and scars, but refuses to leave her abusive husband — and who reminds you of a favorite cousin, who was killed by her abuser. Unless you are aware of what is going on within yourself, your responses to these people won't be based on them and their concerns, but on your emotional responses to someone else in the past. Clearly, that will not help foster genuine or trustworthy relationships with careseekers.

When someone hooks you, what typically happens is that someone does something when interacting with you, and your response is greatly out of proportion to what actually happened. For example, a parishioner drops in to share his "concern" that there were typos in the church newsletter. Instead of simply hearing this as information, or feeling mildly irritated, you find yourself enraged by his complaint. If your emotional response is greatly exaggerated with respect to an actual event, you are probably hooked by something about the other person. When this happens to you, pay attention.

Boundaries[2]

Boundaries have to do with the internal sense of where you end and others begin. They define what is you and what is not you. They tell you what is yours and what is not. They help you figure out what you really are responsible for in life (including ministry) and what is not your responsibility. Above all, boundaries help you to do your work and relate to others and God in healthy and life-giving ways.

There are many kinds of boundaries. Your skin is the most obvious thing that demarcates you from others. Touch, or be touched, and there are implications and meanings, not always positive. Your words — particularly the word "no" — also provide boundaries. Physical space or geographical distance can create boundaries, or you may use emotional distance from someone to create a boundary. Each kind of boundary can function in helpful or unhelpful ways.

Boundaries are not walls, but more like fences with gates in them. When they are healthy, they help people keep good things (for example, feelings of self-esteem, joy, security) inside, and bad things (for example, criticism, judgments, pain) out. When they are damaged or unhealthy, they may function in reverse, keeping the good things out, and letting the bad things in. Boundaries put us in charge of what and who gets into our lives, and what and who is kept out.

People with good boundaries usually have healthy relationships with others. People who have poor boundaries (typically because of childhood experiences) usually do not. They have trouble saying "no" to others and may take on responsibility for others' work or emotions in ways that are inappropriate and draining. They may feel used, disrespected, and exploited by others. They may have trouble recognizing their own needs, asking for help, or letting other people get close emotionally.

They also usually have trouble respecting others' boundaries. They may become very controlling, disrespect limits that others set, or try to manipulate or force others into doing what they want. They may project responsibility for their own life onto others, or may become emotionally unresponsive and incapable of intimacy.

In ministry and in life you are likely to encounter such people. They may ask or demand things of you that are inappropriate, or become angry when you set a boundary with them. For example, a colleague had a parishioner who would call him at home at night and on weekends. When he finally told her that in the future he would only take calls from her during work hours at the church, she resigned her church membership in a fury. Parish pastors in particular may find it challenging to set boundaries with parishioners, who often expect ministers to be available 24/7, and to prioritize parishioners' needs over anything else.

You may also need to work on your own boundaries. Each issue just described can apply to ministers as well as to careseekers. Pastors often have trouble saying "no" or setting limits around their availability. They may have trouble distinguishing the call of their faith to *serve* others with the call to *do everything for* others, even when those others could, and should, do things for themselves. Realistically, this kind of overfunctioning is not helpful for care-receivers since it encourages them to be dependent and to feel ineffective or powerless.

It also takes a huge toll on ministers. When they inappropriately take on others' emotional pain, problems, or responsibilities they end up overworked, resentful, and exhausted. They may become controlling in their work setting and at home. They are also prime candidates for committing sexual misconduct or other forms of pastoral abuse. For all these reasons, it is essential that you be aware of the health and maintenance both of your own boundaries and of those to whom you minister.

The good news is that boundaries can be learned, repaired, or improved, even in adults. While it would have been easier to have learned them earlier, they can still be built. By drawing on the help of appropriate support people and on that of the God who yearns for your wholeness, you can build strong, healthy boundaries that will serve you well in ministry and in your personal life.

Staying Whole

If you ask people who have been in ministry for a while how they are doing, they often say things like "I'm really tired," "I'm not sleeping so well these days," or "I'm wondering if I'm still called to this work." While urging those they care for to make healthy, life-giving choices, too often pastors forget to care for themselves.

Pastoral care is often enjoyable, frequently rewarding, and always challenging, demanding, and ultimately tiring. If we are doing it well, we draw upon our deepest physical, mental, and spiritual reserves, over and over again. So, if we are going to do this work long-term, it is essential that we tend our bodies,[3] minds, and spirits, as well as tending those of careseekers.

Your Spiritual Reservoir

You may have been taught, like many ministers, that if you are willing to serve God and to open yourself to God's Spirit, it will flow effortlessly from God through you to the people you serve.

One problem with this idea is that it doesn't explain very well why some of the most "open" and willing ministers in the world eventually grow exhausted, depleted, and spiritually ill. Despite their efforts and their willingness, they begin to wonder what is wrong with them and why God isn't showing up in the same ways that God used to. They wonder why the work is so hard and draining if they are truly called to do it.

I was one of those people. I graduated from seminary believing my main responsibility as a minister was to be open to the Spirit, and that God would provide all the resources needed to do the work. Ten years later, I was also one of the people asking the hard questions about myself and my ministry. I was very tired, and running close to empty in every part of my life.

Discovering Jane Vennard's beautiful alternative image of this process was a great relief:

> I have often heard the expression that we are to become channels of God's love. I understand this to mean that we are not supposed to be the source of love, but rather we are to clear and empty ourselves so divine love can come through us. However, if we look at the metaphor closely,

it holds us to a constant readiness for God's love to flow through us, with no chance to pause and experience that love for ourselves. I prefer to think that we are called to be reservoirs of God's love, allowing ourselves to be filled and then sharing it with others from our abundance.[4]

Barbara Brown Taylor reflects on a related misconception shared by many pastoral caregivers.[5] She notes that many church workers think that because they are in ministry, because they are trying so hard to do God's work, God will automatically fill them back up again whenever their spiritual gas tanks (reservoirs) start running low. But God doesn't seem to work that way. We have the responsibility to refill our own tanks, lest we find ourselves out of gas and eventually unable to serve anyone else. But how do we do this?

A Nourishing Prayer Life

Praying for yourself is just as essential as praying for others. Whatever form of ministry you are in, you must find ways to intentionally connect with God, to "root [yourself] in the love and mercy of God."[6]

Reflect on what it is that you need to sustain yourself in your work. If you have trouble praying alone, find a prayer community for yourself. Find a prayer form that connects your heart and your spirit with the Holy. Investigate what it means to play and to laugh with God. Learn how work for justice and peace is a form of prayer. However you choose to engage with God, "Praying for ourselves opens our hearts to God's grace, renews our spirits, and gives us the courage to continue our work in the world."[7]

A Community of Nurture

Creating a nurturing life outside of ministry is crucial. Many who go into this work do so with both the expectation and the hope that the work will be their whole life. Because they see it as holy work (and it is), it seems perfectly reasonable to devote their whole mind, body, soul, and strength to it. But studies of effective ministry have found that if ministers do not have real, healthy, whole lives outside of ministry, they are poorer ministers and human beings. Those who serve God best appear to be those who value and enjoy rich relationships outside of their work as well.

We do well to tend to our family relationships with the same deep love and compassion and enthusiasm we bring to our parish work. Families should not always take a back seat to the people in the parish, the patients at the hospital, or the clients served by the nonprofit agency for which we work. A daughter's soccer game, a son's school play, or a spouse's worries about the ill health of a parent should not routinely take a back seat when something "really important" comes up at work. We take the time to do what is most important to us. Let's be sure our families are high on that list.

Ministers also need friends. Since ethical considerations prohibit having close personal friendships with those you serve, we must find a circle of friends outside of our work setting. We all need friends with whom to play or just hang out, and we need soul friends who can hear us in our deepest longings and hold us in our hardest struggles.

Finally, it is immensely helpful to have a support group of people, preferably in a related line of work, with whom we can share some of our concerns and interests, people who are willing to meet regularly to provide support and professional supervision for each other. One of the great blessings in my life is a group of clergywomen with whom I meet once a month, under the supervision of a trained therapist, to offer one another clinical supervision, support, prayer, encouragement, and often gales of laughter. If you can't find such a group, you might think of starting one.

Special Interests

We all need activities in our lives outside of our ministries that invigorate, inspire, refresh, and transform us. We need passions in life that nudge us to continue to learn, move us to new places of creativity, and help us continue to become the full, whole human beings God yearns for us to be. Having those passions — and sharing them with others — can completely transform our ministry.

I have always had hobbies. I was a hand-spinner and weaver for nearly twenty years, and then learned to make pottery. But the real transformation in my life happened several years ago, when after a forty-year wait my childhood dream of owning my own horse became a reality.

In the fall of 2005, a black mare named Bella became part of our household. Her name means "beautiful," and she helps me connect deeply with the beauty of the world. The time I spend with her, feeding, grooming, riding, and caring for her, brings precious treasures into my life.

Sometimes Bella stories make it into my children's sermons, or even into my adult sermons, which both kids and grown-ups seem to enjoy. Through the time I spend with Bella I have become a more deeply grounded, faithful, loving, and whole person, minister, and pastoral caregiver.

What is it that you have longed to do? What would enrich, energize, and relax you? Find something in life outside of work that will stretch you, nurture you, transform you, and help you "grow in holiness."

Time Away

If those to whom you minister know that you care for them, they won't want you to leave them — even for your regular weekly day off, scheduled study leave, or vacations. But beware: if you have tendencies toward codependence,[8] you can delude yourself into thinking that your parishioners or patients or clients can't manage without you, or that if you really were a good minister you wouldn't "abandon them" this way. Do not give up the time that you *must* have away from them in order to thrive. Take your weekly day off, take your vacation days, and take your study leave, if you have it. This time away keeps you healthy physically, mentally, and spiritually. If you don't take it, you will become tired, then depressed, then irritable and angry, and gradually more and more ineffective until you are burned out and of little use to yourself or others.

If you can, get physically away from the setting in which you serve. Tahiti is good, but failing that at least get out of town, away from home, and away from the phone. Take advantage of caller ID to screen calls. Make it clear that when you are "off," you are not available (except, perhaps, for emergencies).

Spiritual Practicing

In order to nurture others' spiritual well-being you need to nurture your own. Engage in whatever spiritual practices nurture your soul, perhaps scriptural exploration through contemplative methods like *lectio divina* (as distinct from "Bible study," which moves this practice from the rest and rejuvenation realm to the work realm), spiritual journaling, walking a labyrinth, or spiritual dancing. Try doing a daily *examen* or guided meditation. Find a spiritual director to support you in your journey.

I have found it enlivening to try spiritual "practicing outside the lines." For example, many people know how to journal in writing, and they find it very helpful. But have you ever considered journaling with a pad of art paper and crayons, or a paint brush in hand? Or with a big damp lump of fresh clay, or a pile of brightly colored fabrics? If you journal in writing, know that you don't have to follow someone's rule that "you should journal every day" but that you can journal whenever you feel like it, which may be once every six months. When it comes to spiritual practices, there are no rules set in stone. Create a practice that you enjoy enough to engage in regularly, and that feeds and refreshes your soul.

Professional Support People

Having some kind of clinical supervision is most helpful. Here I am talking not about oversight of your job performance; rather, a clinical supervisor offers clarity and feedback on issues that you are struggling with in your work. For example, if you find yourself hooked by a parishioner or you are having difficulty setting boundaries with a careseeker, a clinical supervisor can help you work through those issues in a healthy, productive way.

Perhaps you can find a psychotherapist or social worker attuned to faith issues who can provide you with such supervision. This is one case where clergy colleagues are not your best choice. It is more helpful to have someone objective, with no other agenda than the goal of helping you do your work better.

You may also need to find a source of mental health support for yourself. Depression and addictions are extremely common among caregivers, including ministers. If you find yourself experiencing either these or other forms of mental ill health, get help at once. If you feel too exposed by seeking a therapist in the community where you live, find someone elsewhere. Colleagues or the local hospital can offer recommendations.

Summary

As a pastoral caregiver, the greatest gift you can offer another is that of your full presence. It is a presence grounded in faith, in love, in wisdom, and in willingness to serve the God who calls us. It is a presence that draws upon physical, intellectual, and emotional vitality and skills.

Maintaining a healthy pastoral presence requires great self-awareness. Ongoing self-care is also crucial. Such self-care should be considered a spiritual discipline, just like prayer or anything else you do to nurture your relationship with the Holy.

And what about that family we met at the beginning of this chapter in which the mother had died of breast cancer: how might one work with them? We return to them in chapter 8, as we consider issues to do with dying, death, and bereavement. For now, they, and you, are safe in God's hands.

Notes

1. John O'Donohue, *Anam Cara: A Book of Celtic Wisdom* (New York: Cliff Street Books, 1997), xvi–xvii.

2. As with many topics in this text, you need to know far more about boundaries than we can cover here. The Resources section (see page 132 below) offers suggestions for places you can read in greater depth about these topics, and I encourage you to do so.

3. Many available resources offer good information about healthy eating and exercise. You are encouraged to find and read them, and follow their advice. In the rest of this chapter, we focus primarily on emotional and spiritual self-care.

4. Jane E. Vennard, *Embracing the World: Praying for Justice and Peace* (San Francisco: Jossey-Bass, 2003), 67.

5. Barbara Brown Taylor, *Leaving Church* (New York: HarperCollins Publishers, 2006).

6. Vennard, *Embracing the World*, 56.

7. Ibid.

8. Codependence is another crucial concept for pastors to understand. If it is unfamiliar to you, see Resources, page 132 below.

Chapter Four

Hearing Others into Speech

Whenever two or three are gathered . . . I am there. . . .
(Matthew 18:20)

WHEN TWO OR THREE are gathered, whether in a pastor's office, on a mission trip, or at a nursing home tea, they are usually speaking and listening to one another. Scripture reminds us that Jesus Christ is also present with us at those times. Conversation then, is about creating, honoring, and living our relationship with one another, with Christ, and with God.

Pastoral care nearly always entails conversation. Whether you are visiting a patient in the hospital, trying to console someone who has just lost a beloved life partner, or celebrating a teenager's confirmation, in most pastoral care settings someone is speaking and someone else (usually the pastor) is listening. And, because it is pastoral care you are offering, you are listening in a particular way.

Theologian Nelle Morton describes this special kind of listening as "hearing (others) into speech."[1] What she means is that when you listen pastorally, you listen in a way that invites, encourages, and helps others tell their story. Only when you know that story can you help or care for them in the way they most need care. Only when you know how God fits into their story that can you help them reconnect with the Holy in a way that offers healing and hope.

The Leaf Man

Imagine that you are new in your pastoral role in your parish. Maybe you have just been called to this position, or you have just been consecrated as a care partner or Stephen minister. The senior pastor calls and asks you to visit a man named Carroll who is a longtime church member but hasn't attended worship recently.

You drive to Carroll's house, and as you park, you see a man who appears to be in his eighties raking leaves in the front yard. He is tall and thin, and his shoulders stoop a little. He looks up and nods briefly, then goes back to raking.

Pause now to think about what you might do in this situation. What might be helpful for you to notice about Carroll or about the setting? How might you open your conversation? What is happening inside you that might help or hinder the flow of your visit? How might your answers to these questions be different if Carroll were younger? Or female? Or from a different ethnic or racial background than your own? Keep your answers in mind as we explore the nature of pastoral conversations and the skills needed to facilitate them.

Why Listen This Way?

While I was a seminary student, I spent a year working as a hospital chaplain. After returning to school, I had coffee with a friend who was just beginning her student pastorate in a local church. She had been asked to do a hospital visit the next day, which she had never done before. Since I'd worked in a hospital, she wanted me to tell her what to do.

I explained some general principles for making hospital visits, to which she listened impatiently, and then demanded, "But what do I *say?*" She wanted to know exactly what she should say and ask as she made her visit. And that, of course, wasn't something I could tell her. What you say in a pastoral conversation depends largely on what happens while you are with the other person. It is not something that can be planned in advance, but arises out of the moment, although of course it is grounded in your theological and spiritual assumptions and beliefs.

How you converse in these situations depends in part on what you are trying to accomplish. Your first goal in the conversation with Carroll is that of any pastoral care encounter: to begin to develop a relationship. Once you have done that, you will know better what care he needs, and later conversations will be oriented around that care.

With Carroll, as with many care-receivers, at least part of your work together will likely involve healing. As one author puts it, "[Pastoral] ministry is . . . a kind of partnership with the divine for bringing about wholeness."[2] You partner with God to bind up the broken-hearted, help those who are in despair find hope, and assist those who are ill in body, mind, or spirit to reclaim the abundant healthy life that God yearns for us to have. Sometimes healing involves solving hard problems or finding new ways to respond to difficult life situations. Often it includes reclaiming and honoring one's sacred human wholeness. And nearly always it entails "the restoration and transformation of the full human being in his or her relationships."[3]

When you enter into conversation with another person, by that very act you begin the healing process. Meg Wheatley reminds us, "Listening creates relationship. . . . Everybody has a story, and everybody wants to tell their story in order to connect. . . . In the English language, the word for *health* comes from the same root as the word for *whole*. We can't be healthy if we're not in relationship. And *whole* is from the same root word as *holy*. Listening moves us closer. It helps us become more whole, more healthy, more holy."[4] So, your pastoral conversations with others help them become more whole, and reconnect them with the human family and with God.

Being a Nonanxious Presence

Before one can listen to others in a whole and holy way, one must be fully present. We began to explore this in chapter 3. Here we consider what it means to be a "nonanxious presence."

That may sound daunting, especially for those of us who do feel anxious about doing pastoral care. Those feelings are normal. They are also healthy, because they help us pay closer attention to this sacred and challenging new work we are doing.

Being a nonanxious presence does not mean that we suppress our feelings or somehow learn to never feel anxious. It means learning how to be with others in such a way that our anxiety doesn't interfere with our ability to act pastorally, which may include helping others manage their own anxiety.

For example, early in her ministry, a pastor was asked to perform a "small home wedding" for a couple who were to be married on New Year's Eve. She met with them for prenuptial work and planned the service, and finally the special evening arrived.

This was her first wedding, and she was extremely nervous when she pulled up in front of a large house where every light was blazing, and about a hundred people were wandering around carrying refreshments. It was not the small gathering or cozy setting she had anticipated.

Nonetheless, she gathered up her *Book of Worship*, clergy robe, and stole, and knocked on the front door. The groom answered, a personable young man who was normally self-assured. But that evening he was white as a sheet and clearly terrified. She took a deep breath and talked quietly with him about his fears. Finally he said to her, "It's a good thing you're calm. If you weren't, I'd totally lose it!"

While she certainly wasn't feeling calm, she had managed to control her own anxiety and be present to him in their conversation. As a result, he was able to grow calmer, reconnect with his joy in why they were there, and enter into the service with a quiet, sure sense of God's grace and presence with him and his bride.

So how do we develop this nonanxious presence? The more practice we have, the less worried we become about doing a particular thing — in this case, ministry. And until you are more practiced, strategies such as breath work, prayer, and meditation can be helpful.

Basic Structure in Pastoral Conversations[5]

There are four basic steps in having effective pastoral conversations. These steps may look and feel different, depending on the circumstances. For example, a quick exchange after the trustees' meeting will be different from a conversation with a person in the hospital recovering from surgery, which will be different from a consultation in your office with a parishioner about her daughter's drug addiction.

Whatever the circumstances, the first step is *coming together.* This step entails beginning to build a partnership so the careseeker knows you are on his or her side. The key goal in this stage is to create an atmosphere of respect, connection, and care.

Creating such an atmosphere may be harder than it sounds. The person who phoned the day before to set an appointment "immediately" suddenly seems unable to talk about anything other than the weather. The couple who urgently told you during coffee hour that they had to see you right away spends twenty minutes talking about their new car. If this happens, take the initiative, perhaps with a question like, "When you spoke with me earlier, it sounded like there was something important that you wanted to talk about."

The second step involves *exploration* as you begin to gather more information about this person, and what brought her or him to you. Careseekers begin to share their stories, and you learn more about their thoughts and feelings about their situations. They also begin to share their theology, and you start to discern how they see God as present or absent in their life. In this step, you are seeking to figure out their real concerns and the kind of help they need.

The third step can only be undertaken once you clearly understand the careseeker's story and theology. Now you move from discerning what is needed to *intervening* — specifically, to helping the careseeker do what is needed. You still listen for thoughts and feelings, but the energy now moves toward taking some kind of action.

At this stage, encourage careseekers to take responsibility for what happens next. As pastoral caregivers, our task is not to fix things for people, even though we may want to do exactly that. Yes, sometimes others will need us to help them help themselves. A person who is severely incapacitated or alone may need us to make phone calls or provide other brief assistance. Usually, though, it is most beneficial for care-receivers to do as much as possible of what needs doing themselves. Your pastoral task is to help careseekers figure out what needs to be done, then provide encouragement and support as they do it.

The fourth and final step involves coming to *closure*. When you visit with friends or chat with someone at a party, you don't usually terminate the conversation by simply walking away. You don't do that in pastoral care settings either. As your time with a careseeker nears its end, you will intentionally bring closure to the conversation. You may want to briefly review what you have talked about and what the next step is. If you have given the careseeker a referral, you may want to review how to contact the person to whom you have referred them. It will almost always be appropriate to end your time together with a prayer. Well-done closure helps the person feel an ongoing connection with you as a concerned pastoral caregiver, with the wider community, and most important, with God.

Some Basic Conversational Skills

Think of a time when someone listened to you in a way that was especially helpful. What about that situation — the nature of their presence, what they said, what they invited you to do — was especially helpful? Now think of a time when someone listened to you in a way that was very unhelpful — perhaps even upsetting. Again, what about that situation made their listening unhelpful? You have probably just identified several things that you should be aware of as you conduct your own pastoral conversations. The following practices will also make you a more effective pastoral conversation partner.

Presence

In chapter 3, we considered at length the concept of pastoral presence. We recalled that it is essential to bring our full selves to the pastoral conversation, to "enter slowly, softly, heart first."[6] Only if we are fully present can we listen well and respond helpfully.

Paying Attention

Learn to listen with your eyes as well as with your ears. When you enter another's space, whether their home, hospital room, or front lawn, notice the person and her or his surroundings. What are her facial expressions? What is his demeanor? Is she clean, dressed, and groomed as she usually is? How is he standing or sitting? Are there objects in the room to which she pays special attention? Is his room tidy or disordered? Is there anything that seems unusual about the setting? Is what the person tells you congruent with the nonverbal messages you receive?

For example, a pastor visited a parishioner in her home. Edna was legally blind and had other chronic health issues, but lived alone, and the pastor's impression was that she usually managed to care for herself quite well. She was always clean and well-dressed when she came to church, and appeared well-nourished and happy. He had chosen to visit this day because he knew that Edna had been ill recently, and he was concerned about her well-being.

When he entered Edna's house, he was struck by the dirt and disorder everywhere. Piles of papers were strewn around the room, dirty clothes were on the floor, and there was a definite odor throughout the house. She greeted him wearing a food-stained dress, and her hair was dirty and unkempt. When she asked him to bring her a glass of water, he noticed the kitchen sink was stacked with unwashed dishes, the floor was sticky, and the refrigerator was nearly empty.

He expressed his concerns to her, and Edna said forcefully that she was "just fine." Yet undertones of sadness in her voice combined with the state of the house told him that she was not. When he gently suggested this, she admitted with clear distress that she had been out of groceries for several days, but hadn't wanted to bother anyone with her needs. She was also feeling ill and dizzy, and had been unable to get out of bed for more than a few minutes at a time.

After talking a while, she agreed to let him bring her some fresh food and to contact her doctor, who scheduled an appointment for Edna the next day. It turned out that her medications were interacting to cause the dizziness and nausea, and once her prescriptions were adjusted, she began to get better immediately. She and her pastor also worked out a plan with two of her friends to check on her regularly in case she had further problems.

Asking Questions

The first instinct most caregivers have when beginning pastoral conversations is to ask questions. Some questions can be useful in learning what we need to know in order to help. However, we can also overuse them, or ask in ways that block rather than widen the conversational flow.

Strive for questions and responses that make space for careseekers to describe their experience. Rather than stating how things are (for example, "That is really hard"), you might instead wonder aloud ("I wonder if that is hard for you?"). Phrases like "it sounds like" (you are feeling sad, you are feeling frustrated) or "it seems as if" (this has been painful for you) are much more helpful than statements suggesting we know how life is for them.

We never know exactly how it is for the other person, and it can be very off-putting to suggest that we do.

Asking open-ended rather than closed questions also facilitates conversations by allowing a person to reflect on what is happening and offering them permission to share their story with us. An open-ended question is one that has many possible answers, such as "How are you feeling today?" or "How did you feel when he said that?" A closed question is rhetorical, or has only one or two possible answers, such as "Are you feeling all right today?" or "Did it make you mad when he said that?" Closed questions impede or stop conversational flow.

Finally, be careful not to interrogate people. Bombarding others with a series of questions feels invasive. Try not to fall into the trap of asking a question, then re-asking it a different way, then pursuing it with yet another question, without giving the other person a chance to answer. This makes people feel unheard, and sometimes defensive and angry. It sets you up as the person in charge, rather than as a partner in healing. Learn to ask, then leave time and space for the person to reflect and answer.

Going Deeper

Perhaps you are familiar with the work of Carl Rogers and his "reflective listening" method for psychotherapy. Rogers's basic approach was to "echo" what the client said, as a way to make the person feel heard. For example, the counselee might say, "I am so mad at my partner's mother, I'd like to scream," and the therapist might respond, "You are really angry."

As the method became more widely used, most counselors and other caregivers found that modified forms of this technique were more helpful. These forms reflect careseekers' comments indirectly, in ways that invite them to go deeper.

Reflection offers a nonjudgmental statement in which you check your understanding of what the other person is saying. Often it involves paraphrasing — restating in your own words — what the person just said. The goal is to clarify what the careseeker is saying, for your sake and theirs. For example, "I hear you saying. . . . Is that correct?" Often the caregiver's reflective responses help careseekers perceive their situations in a whole new way.

Probing includes open-ended comments or requests that invite the other person to expand on what they have already shared. For example, the caregiver can say, "Tell me more about that" or "Help me understand how that works for you." Or, when the person says, "I feel totally out of control," you might respond, "How so?" Probing and reflective responses can be two of the most helpful tools in your pastoral tool kit.

Interpreting is more teaching oriented, and helps care-receivers understand something more clearly. For example, a careseeker might tell you that his new stepson misbehaves in ways that lead to frequent arguments between himself and his new wife. After you clearly understand his situation, it may be helpful for you to explain some things about family dynamics or about blended families. Be careful not to overuse interpretive responses: they shift careseekers' attention from their feelings to their intellects, which makes emotional healing difficult.

Supportive responses are meant to reassure the careseeker. People often worry that any feeling they experience that is not positive and happy is "bad." To a person struggling with anger or depression or other feelings that mainstream culture has come to label as "unhealthy," learning that those feelings are normal can be helpful and can be a step along the road to health and wholeness.

Evaluative responses should be used with caution. These statements impose a judgment about whether we think what the person is doing is good or bad. Most people hear such statements as judgments of themselves — which seldom produces the kind of safe, trusting relationship you are trying to build. For example, if a person going through difficulties in a work situation says, "I'm just going to quit my job!" an evaluative response would be "That's a really good [or bad] idea." While your feedback can sometimes be helpful, it needs to be offered in a nonjudgmental form. In this case, you might try something like "That sounds like one option. What other options have you considered?" This approach will encourage careseekers to reflect more deeply on their situations. In contrast, evaluative responses tend to shut down such reflection.

Advising involves suggesting a course of action for the carereceiver to take, which occasionally is appropriate and helpful. For example, a person who is struggling financially because of frequent spending sprees might benefit from your advice to get some financial counsel. However, assisting careseekers in developing action plans of their own is usually more helpful. A response like "So, what do you think you need to do about this?" is far more helpful than "Here's what you should do."

Your Patterns

As you begin to have pastoral conversations, pay attention to the kinds of responses you use most often. What is most comfortable for you? What is least comfortable? What effects do those different responses have on the people for whom you are caring? How will you practice new responses that will help you more effectively hear them into speech?

More Things to Consider

Self-Disclosure

Your own experiences and feelings can sometimes prompt questions that help the careseeker go deeper. For example, suppose a parishioner describes a problem she is having with her adult son. He won't keep a job, engages in high-risk behaviors, and keeps coming home and asking for money. Suppose this is similar to a problem you encountered with your own child. You know from your experience that the situation she is describing caused you great feelings of frustration and fears about both your child's well-being and your own competence as a parent. Drawing on your experience, you might say something like "It sounds like that is really frustrating for you" or "It sounds like you are worried about his safety" — rather than offering a description of what happened in your own situation.

Sharing personal information with a care-receiver is called "self-disclosure," and it is a controversial issue in the pastoral care and therapeutic communities: when, if ever, is it appropriate for a caregiver to self-disclose personal information?

Self-disclosure is problematic for two reasons. First, it often occurs to meet the caregiver's needs. Second, it confuses boundaries, particularly if careseekers come to feel they need to care for the minister instead of the minister caring for them. Usually self-disclosure should be avoided or minimized in pastoral conversations.

How 'Bout Them Broncos?

I live in Colorado, where the Denver Broncos are the home football team. Over my fourteen years of ministry here, careseekers have initiated many pastoral conversations with questions like the one in this section title. While they really want to talk about their troubled child or failing marriage or health worries, many people aren't able to enter into a pastoral conversation that directly. Instead they start the conversation by asking something apparently quite unrelated.

There are times, of course, when they really do want to talk about the local team — or a recent concert or a community issue — as a way of being in relationship with their minister, and it is helpful for you to be able to talk about those things. Over the course of the conversation, as your relationship deepens, so does their trust in you, which may ultimately make it possible for them to raise deeper, more serious concerns.

When you are talking with someone, especially in a conversation they have initiated, be listening under the surface for what they are really asking or saying. They may need you to invite them to go deeper, to express their real concerns. Or they may just want to know you are a friend who will discuss lighthearted topics as well as serious ones.

Letting Silence Happen

When in the presence of a person in distress, simply letting silence happen is sometimes surprisingly difficult. In our concern to help the other person, we may assail them with questions, or run through our entire repertoire of other pastoral responses to try to get them to say something to which we can then respond.

Sometimes the most helpful thing we can say is nothing. Simply sitting with another, sharing our calm and compassionate presence, knowing that we are both held in God's care, can be immensely healing. We do well to learn to honor the silence in which God may be heard more clearly than is sometimes possible in the midst of noise.

Cultural Awareness

When we listen to people from cultural backgrounds different from our own, it is particularly important not to assume that we understand what they are telling us. In such cases, reflective responses — particularly paraphrasing — can be especially helpful.

How we use questions can spell the difference between care and rudeness. In some cultures, direct questions are considered highly impolite. Some cultures value personal privacy more highly than others, and attempts to go deeper may be perceived as invasive and even hostile.

Carefully and continually checking out our understanding of what the other person is telling us — sometimes nonverbally as well as with their words — is crucial to meaningful conversation. To establish a relationship grounded in trust, be aware of and sensitive to cultural differences in communication styles and practices.

Listening Theologically

One of the distinguishing features of pastoral conversations is that they always occur within a theological framework. As the pastoral caregiver, you remain aware of God's presence with you and the careseeker, and you help them remember that as well. In addition, you are listening throughout the conversation for the signs of their understanding of God, and how that affects the way they are living. The next chapter considers these issues more deeply.

Summary

Pastoral conversations are a three-way event involving the pastoral caregiver, the care-receiver, and God. Acting as God's warmhearted representative, the pastor uses a variety of skills to help careseekers tell their stories. Hearing others into speech in this way is an act of profound healing in and of itself. Simply by listening to the other's story, you bless it with your presence and with God's. You also help speakers unfold their stories in new ways, often discovering new meanings even as they tell you (and God) what is happening in their lives.

Notes

1. Nelle Morton, *The Journey Is Home* (Boston: Beacon Press, 1986).

2. Rodney J. Hunter, "The Therapeutic Tradition of Pastoral Care and Counseling," in Pamela D. Couture and Rodney J. Hunter, eds., *Pastoral Care and Social Conflict* (Nashville: Abingdon, 1995), 19.

3. Ibid.

4. Margaret J. Wheatley, *Turning to One Another: Simple Conversations to Restore Hope to the Future* (San Francisco: Berrett-Koehler Publishers, 2002), 89–90.

5. Material in this section is based on Harry Stack Sullivan's suggestions in *The Psychiatric Interview* (New York: W. W. Norton, 1980). While Sullivan's focus is on therapeutic situations, his general guidelines are directly applicable to many kinds of pastoral conversations.

6. Karyn D. Kedar, *Our Dance with God: Finding Prayer, Perspective, and Meaning in the Stories of Our Lives* (Woodstock, VT: Jewish Lights Publishing, 2004), 29.

Chapter Five

Godward Listening

The best of human listening (involves) a preciously thin membrane where the human and divine can be felt to mingle.... The living Listener's presence may almost imperceptibly rise into awareness and with that awareness the total situation is altered.[1]

TEACHERS OFFER GUIDANCE to students. Therapists sustain clients through hard times. Medical professionals aid healing. Social workers facilitate reconciliation. All these listen to others' deepest concerns and respond out of wisdom and compassion. Their work reflects four key facets of the work called pastoral care. Yet typically their work is not considered to be "ministry," nor are their conversations considered "pastoral" listening.

Two features set pastoral listening apart from other kinds of helpful hearing and responding. First, it arises out of a theological grounding. Second, it arises in part from the caregiver's relationship with God. Together these call forth, expand, and sometimes challenge the theological understandings of those to whom care is provided.

Pastoral listening helps careseekers experience that mingling of the human and the Holy referred to in the quotation above. It involves communicating God to others, through words and actions, and helping make God visible through God-reflecting acts of care.

Pastoral Listening as a Theological Act

In chapter 1, we considered some of the theological assumptions that underlie pastoral care. These assumptions mean that as *pastoral* caregivers we bring a certain perspective to each care-giving encounter — one framed by and grounded in our "words about God." We come as visible representatives of the Invisible One in whom we live and move and have our being. And we come within the context of a community that understands itself to be part of the body of Christ.

Pastoral encounters take place with a conscious awareness that there is a third partner who is always part of the interchange. Pastoral caregivers know that they are not just having a conversation with another person, but that both they and the careseeker are also having a conversation with God or in the presence of God. When we listen and speak together that way, we are conversing theologically, engaging in what one author calls "Godward listening."[2] When we engage in Godward listening we listen to others and to the events of our own life with one ear turned toward God.

The Hospital Patient

Some years ago I served as a hospital chaplain. One Saturday night I was paged to the oncology unit to see a patient. Craig was in his mid-fifties and had pancreatic cancer. His doctor had just seen him and told him the cancer was progressing rapidly and he probably did not have much longer to live.

As we talked, I learned that Craig's chief concern was not his pain or fears about his death, but a long-past broken relationship with his son. Two decades earlier, they had had a serious fight over the direction the son's life was taking and had broken off their relationship. Craig had not seen his son since. On this night he wanted to talk with a minister because he feared that "God could never forgive him for what he had done to his son."

Being very new in ministry, and deeply aware of his obvious pain, I completely forgot about letting God participate in our conversation. Instead, I rushed in to reassure Craig that of course God loved him and forgave him. Then — without taking time to reflect together on what God might have to say to us — I prayed with him, and left the room feeling like I had done a pretty good job of pastoral care.

When I brought the case to my clinical supervision group, they offered a different perspective. One person asked why I was so unwilling to let Craig make his confession and struggle with his feelings about that. Another asked why I hadn't explored with him *his* understanding of God, rather than telling him mine. Another wondered whether it might have been worthwhile to explore with Craig how he understood forgiveness. Clearly, there was much theological reflection we could have done that might have been helpful.

It was an invaluable learning experience for me. I realized how important it is to intentionally make space for God's presence and voice in pastoral interactions. I learned that helping careseekers voice their theological concerns and convictions is more important than voicing mine. And I discovered that it is important to extend grace not only to others but also to ourselves when we are learning to do something new, like pastoral care.

Knowing Your Theology

Lawrence Holst suggests that "care becomes uniquely pastoral when it helps to direct others to the source of life and power, to that which alone is infinite and eternal."[3] Caregivers need to have as clear a sense as possible of how they understand that Source, and that which is "infinite and eternal." That is, caregivers need to know their own theology — what their "words about God" are, and why they believe those words are true.

This does not mean having all the answers. With something as mysterious and magnificent as God and faith, no one does, but it means knowing what you believe about theological issues like grace, sin, trust, grief, and hope, and reflecting on how those issues arise in human situations like marriage, sexuality, conflict, and loss. And knowing your own theology means continually working to connect your faith understandings and your lived experience, and helping careseekers do the same.

Many of us often feel inadequate in this area of pastoral care. Just as some caregivers hesitate to use biblical sources in caregiving because they feel they "don't know the Bible," some hesitate to address theological issues because they feel they "don't know their theology." Yet each of us does know our theology whether or not we are yet able to articulate it to others.

Imagine that you order some Girl Scout cookies from a youth at your church. When the cookies are left at your office, you discover three more boxes than you paid for. You immediately pick up the phone, call the cookie seller, and offer to either return the extra cookies or pay for them.

Why did you make that call? You could easily have kept the extra cookies and enjoyed the unexpected bonus, yet when confronted with this dilemma, you made a choice to do the right thing based on your faith values and beliefs. While you probably didn't consciously analyze how your theology of justice or right relationship was relevant here, you acted in a certain way because of your theological understandings.

Our challenge, then, is to learn to reflect on and articulate what we believe and why. As we do, the way we respond to careseekers will become as automatically and genuinely grounded in our theology as our response to the Girl Scout.

In part, this ability develops as we nurture our own relationship with God. We have already considered the importance of prayer and other spiritual practices in deepening our connections with the Holy. In part, our theological maturation happens through deliberate study and reflection. Read and study the Scriptures. Take courses in theology, if possible. Read seriously in the areas of theology and ethics. Critically reflect on tensions between the value systems prevalent in the wider culture and those of faith communities. Discern what sources of authority are important for you as you explore different viewpoints and determine which of those govern your faith, your life, and the way you offer care.

There is no one right way to work on developing your theological framework. You will figure out as you go along what works best for you. Some situations may still catch you by surprise. But if you have done your work, when you need that clear knowing of your "words about God," it will be there. It will shape what you say and do, and help you provide the most faithful and valuable care possible.

Talking about God

To do pastoral care, we need to be able to talk about God without getting embarrassed. While obvious, perhaps, it is not as simple as it sounds. Talking about God well takes a lot of practice, a lot of willingness, and a lot of courage given our culture. Talking about God as if we take God seriously puts us at risk of looking foolish or decidedly out of touch with today's world.

Even so, we *must* talk of God when we are doing pastoral care. That, after all, is why careseekers have asked to talk with us and not, say, a social worker. It is not simply because we are readily available, or because our fees are low, or that we can offer the same kind of psychological help they could receive from a therapist. They come to us because we symbolize the One whose presence they are most yearning to feel in the midst of their pain or confusion or struggles. And they come assuming that even if they aren't comfortable speaking about God or using theological language, we are. They come hoping that we will be able to lead them to new places in their understanding of the way God works in the world, particularly in their world. They come yearning for us to help them connect in a new way with the Holy. To accomplish any of this, we must be able to talk about God.

A Method for Pastoral Assessment

There is an old saw in the pastoral care community that when all else fails in pastoral conversation, you can always ask, "So where do you see God in all of this?" And most of the time that really *is* what careseekers most want to discover. Yet while the question can be both appropriate and useful at times, there are some issues to explore with careseekers that will help them answer that ultimate question in the context of their particular situations. The process by which we explore these issues is called pastoral (or spiritual) assessment.

Spiritual caregivers today are blessed with a wealth of tools for conducting such assessments. Here we focus on Paul Pruyser's approach,[4] since it remains one of the most useful models available.

Pruyser was a clinician who was interested in intersections between faith and living. He developed a framework that helps caregivers explore connections between careseekers' stated theologies and their actual lived experiences. Assessing the following seven dimensions of experience can help you discern what kind of help careseekers require.[5]

Awareness of the Holy

This dimension involves how the person thinks and feels about the Holy. What does this person center his life around? Does she have a sense of something larger than herself in the universe? What does he revere or respect? How does she experience reverence or awe? What is the central value in this person's life?

Since many careseekers equate the Holy with God, explore with them how they understand God. For them, what are God's defining attributes? Do they see God primarily as close and present, or as distant and detached? As mostly loving and supportive, or as judgmental and punitive? How do they understand the relationship between Jesus and God, and do they relate more to one or the other? How does the Holy Spirit function for them? How does their actual behavior relate to these understandings?

Faith

For Pruyser, this has to do with how a person subjectively experiences and lives his or her religious understandings. What is

the careseeker committed to, and how does it shape his or her response to the world? What guides her investments of time, energy,
and gifts? When and how does he engage with something bigger
than himself?

In this context, faith is not something a person either does
or does not have. It is a complex set of beliefs and attitudes toward both the sacred and the world that shapes the connections
people make between the two. A person's faith may be clarified
by exploring the dimensions below.

Sense of Providence

Theologically, determining a careseeker's sense of providence has
to do with how he or she understands "the Divine Presence's
intention toward himself or herself."[6] It includes careseekers' questions about whether God has a plan for their life, and what kind
of plan it might be. How do they understand trust? Do they sense
that the world is a friendly and safe place for them to live, or do
they see the world as threatening and dangerous?

Persons who have had traumatic experiences often do not have
a positive sense of providence. Those who have experienced neglect or abuse may have difficulty imagining that anyone, even
God, might care about them. Those who have been harmed by
others may not trust anybody, including God. It may be hard
for these people to summon hope, or to imagine that things
could become better. In contrast, people with a positive sense of
providence are usually hopeful and open to growth and change.

Vocation

This dimension has to do with how people see themselves fitting
in to the larger scheme of things in the world. Do they have a
sense of purpose or meaning in life? Do they believe that the way
they are using their physical, emotional, and spiritual resources in
the world is effective? Do they feel that what they are doing with
their life matters? Do they have a sense of zest and passion for
life, or do they feel drained and empty?

People who feel that their lives have meaning, that what they do matters, generally have more resources to draw on when they are in the midst of hard situations. Those who question the worth of what they do and how they live, especially those who see few options for change, may feel helpless and despairing in the face of difficulty.

Grace or Gratefulness

This dimension has to do with a sense of God's graciousness, of what blessings are and where they come from, and with the sense of how to respond to the good things in one's life. Is the careseeker genuinely grateful? If so, for what? If not, what makes it difficult for them to feel grateful? How do they understand God's grace, and the relationship of that to works righteousness? Where do they see themselves called to extend grace to others?

People whose lives have been especially difficult, or who were raised in homes where harshness prevailed, may have difficulty believing that God's grace is for them, too. Learning to sense that grace can be the beginning of profound healing for them.

Sin, Repentance, and Forgiveness

Millions of pages have been written about the meaning of sin. Here, let us think about it as brokenness in one's relationship with God. When people think about sin, they typically focus on things they have done that they believe were wrong. Traditionally, when people recognize their sins, the call of faith is to repent, which involves feeling remorse and changing one's behavior in the future, to restore right relationship with the Holy.

When assessing this, the pastor explores with careseekers their sense of responsibility for their actions, their understandings of the consequences their actions have, and their ability to change direction in the way they are living. How do they understand what it means to sin? What, if any, is their sense of guilt related to their behavior? Do they take responsibility for their mistakes? Can they change direction (repent) when they discover they have erred? What is their sense of God's forgiveness?

Community or Communion

This last dimension regards the person's sense of connection to the network of human relationships. This may occur through family, vocational commitments, social circles, a faith community, or some other setting where a sense of being part of the human family is present. The sense of connection is reflected in their sense of themselves as being in touch with others, or as isolated and alone.

Part of this sense of connection includes their coming to visit you, but beyond you, where else is this person embedded? With whom do they have relationships, and what kinds of relationships do they have? Where can they reach out and know they are cared for? Where are they estranged from the world? What individuals or groups support them in their struggles?

From a caregiving perspective, this is one of the most important dimensions to assess, since people who have good support networks are much more likely to heal, recover, and flourish than those who do not. Encouraging or helping careseekers connect with others is one of the most important things we can do.

Applying the Model

Applying Pruyser's model to my interaction with Craig, here is what I noticed: Craig's image of God was as a remote, judgmental figure. Craig's sense of his faith was tied to church attendance; since he had not attended for many years, he characterized his faith as "pretty weak." He wondered about the meaning his life had had, but described it as having been "pretty good, overall." He felt he had generally been "blessed," with a good marriage and work he had enjoyed.

Clearly there was a strong contrast between that positive sense of providence and grace and Craig's fears of God's judgment and wrath. Exploring that disconnect with him, and of his understandings of forgiveness, would probably have been very helpful for him. It would also have been useful to have reflected with him on his community of support as he faced the end of his life. While Craig clearly had good professional caregivers, a broader support network might have blessed him in other ways.

It's Not That Simple

Pastoral caregiving would be a lot easier if we could just memorize the list above and use it as a checklist with each careseeker to determine where they are theologically and what kind of assistance they most need. The reality of pastoral care is that people's lives are far too complex to fit into such neat categories. So while the seven dimensions in Pruyser's model offer us a helpful starting place, there are yet more issues to attend to as you engage in Godward listening.

Speaking To or Speaking For

In some way, pastoral care involves the communication of the word of God. Exactly what that communication looks like often depends on the caregiver's faith tradition.

In the early Christian church and in some traditions today, the caregiver's primary responsibility was thought to be speaking the word of God *to* careseekers. This practice assumes that caregivers know more about the Bible, theology, and God than careseekers do, and should use that greater knowledge to guide careseekers into the correct path for living.

In other traditions today, the caregiver's task is seen as listening for the word of God *with* careseekers. This practice takes into account both the caregiver's and the careseeker's understandings of God, Scripture, and how faith calls us to live. It is grounded in the belief that God speaks equally clearly to those who offer and those who receive help. Listening with careseekers involves calls to listen and wait for the word of God. As Howard Stone notes, our waiting "can change for the better many aspects of the care being offered today. Our care need not be so frenzied, so doing-oriented, so worried. Though as pastors we do everything we can to help others, ultimate care comes as a gift from the outside.... Faith involves the assurance that God's Word *will* come, but not the knowledge of when or how."[7]

To offer effective care, we need to know our tradition's stance on this issue, as well as our own. Then we need to develop the knowledge and skills required to work effectively within the model we embrace.

Silence or Speech

In pastoral caregiving, what is often the caregiver's greatest gift can also become the greatest barrier to letting God work. Most people who enter the helping professions, especially ministry, are very good with words. Words have inspired them, nurtured them, and come easily to them. Unfortunately, in caregiving situations words can create so much noise that it becomes hard for caregivers and careseekers to hear God's voice.

In my encounter with Craig, though my goal was to offer him comfort and support, I became so caught up in what I wanted to say that there was little space for him to speak, or for either of us to listen to God. I learned then, and have rediscovered many times since, that sometimes silence can be far more pastoral and helpful than speech.

It is natural, when faced with a person in pain, to want to reassure them. When we believe deeply in a God who cares, we want to remind those who suffer that God cares for them. Sometimes we feel compelled to fill silence with sound. Yet God often speaks "in a still, small voice," and our pastoral task becomes making space and being quiet so that that voice can be perceived.

Accepting or Confronting

There will be times in your caregiving when the person to whom you are offering care will express a very different theology from your own. This is especially true if you offer care to persons from a variety of faith backgrounds, as do most hospital chaplains, hospice workers, and spiritual directors. Even parish pastors who care mainly for their own congregation are sometimes surprised by theological statements that some members make in situations of distress.

Imagine that you are called to the emergency room of your local hospital late one Saturday night. A young man has been badly hurt in a truck rollover accident, and his family has just arrived at the hospital. As you join them, the father jumps up and says, "Well, I guess this is God's way of teaching him not to drink a case of beer and then jump into that old truck of his!"

If your theological assumptions are different from his, you may be tempted to contradict or challenge him. For example, you might say, "No, God doesn't work that way." It is more helpful instead to draw him out and explore with him how he understands God's activity in what has happened, or you may simply support him spiritually without either agreeing or disagreeing with him.

How you respond will depend partly on your understanding of your responsibility to "speak the word to" or "listen for the word with" the careseeker. It will also depend on the particular situation at hand. In general, if careseekers are in great pain, fear, or distress, it is *not* the time to challenge them on their theological views. Instead, a more neutral response — for example, "At times like this, I wonder why these things happen, too" — can validate their questioning and struggle without violating your integrity or assaulting their beliefs. You might also offer to call their pastor to come and comfort them. Finally, you can simply support them by your presence and prayers.

Language Matters

Any time we "talk theology," especially when we are engaged in Godward listening, the words we use to embody our faith understandings and to reflect those of the careseeker matter deeply.

They can nurture, heal, and expand the careseeker's relationship with God, or they can hinder, constrict, even damage that person's faith experience.

Because this issue is so crucial to offering good pastoral care, I recommend several practices. Do some Bible study to discover and appreciate the remarkable variety of ways in which God is described (for example, Gen. 3:21; Deut. 32:18; Isa. 40:18, 25; Jer. 31:20; Ps. 22:9; and Matt. 6:30). Read some of the resources listed for chapter 5 on pp. 133–40. Learn how the ways the church has referred to God have changed over the centuries. We often assume the language used today for God is the way it has always been, which is an inaccurate assumption. The God we worship and serve as a living God is reflected by the language we use to describe God, perhaps particularly in the way we image God's gender. While many people still image God as a male figure, a growing number have begun to view God in more expansive ways. This expanding awareness of the array of biblical images for God, and how these images affect persons' relationships with God, have led people of both sexes to describe God with imagery and pronouns beyond the masculine and the hierarchical.

Though you may opt not to change the way you image or refer to God, a broadened understanding of and appreciation for others' images of God will make you a more respectful and helpful caregiver.

A second area where language matters has to do with culture. Pastoral caregivers who are part of the dominant culture in the United States may make theological assumptions people from other cultural groups do not share. For example, if you were raised in Sunday schools that prominently displayed pictures of a blond, blue-eyed Jesus, your internalized image of Jesus may be quite different from someone raised in a different cultural setting who grew up with pictures of Jesus as dark-skinned and dark-haired.

Presbyterian theologian Hyung Kyung Chung shares this helpful example:

As a theological student I always thought God was a spirit and not an image. But I had an image of God as a Caucasian man with blue eyes, long hair, with a big nose and a white robe. My intellectual side said, "God has no image. God is spirit." But all my upbringing as a Christian in Korea in a Korean church that was founded by Western missionaries, all my Sunday school education, was based on this picture of God who looks like Moses in the movie *The Ten Commandments.*

Through a long personal struggle I realized one day that my image of God is like a middle-aged Korean woman looking like my mother — very warm, affirming, available, strong, and "down to earth." When I pray, this image comes to me. . . . It's very liberating because before, when I prayed to God who was white, who was old, who was a man, it was difficult for me to feel connected with him.[8]

We caregivers do well not to make assumptions about others' theology, including their images of the Holy, but to listen carefully for what and how careseekers believe, and how they live into their understandings of those things they hold most sacred. Using similar theological language, if you can do so with integrity, will deepen the level of conversational meaning for careseekers, and will enhance both their and your ability to listen Godward.

The Action-Reflection Model

Not only does and should your theology shape the care you give, but that care should also shape your theology. This is referred to as the "action-reflection model" for pastoral caregiving, meaning that you take a pastoral care action with someone, pay attention to what happens, and reflect on the experience afterward. You then use your reflection to decide whether to use that practice again in the future, or instead do something different — not simply because what you did felt right or "worked," but because you know it was also theologically sound.

For example, in my hospital encounter with Craig, I entered the situation, attempted to offer comfort, and spoke words of grace. My colleagues' feedback helped me realize that I could have done other things to help Craig with his theological questions. I reflected on their feedback and how it connected with my theological conviction that God is always speaking to us and calling us to new ways of being. The next time I encountered a patient struggling with issues similar to Craig's, I tried a new approach, which included helping that person struggle with issues of repentance and forgiveness.

To become an increasingly better pastoral caregiver, this action-reflection approach is essential. We are transformed by taking in our experiences in caregiving, thinking about them, praying with them, then connecting them in new ways to our stores of practical knowledge and our theology.

Summary

Truly pastoral care is grounded in our understandings of and our relationships with God. Listening with others for God, how we invite God into each pastoral care situation, and how we talk together about God depend on our theology and the theology of the careseeker. To become more effective as caregivers, we therefore continually deepen our own theological understandings as well as help careseekers discern God's presence in whatever is happening in their lives.

As we communicate God to and with those in our care, may we be aware of the complexities of this process, mindful of the language we and they use to describe the Holy, and attentive, as always, to cultural differences. All of these things help us bring "the living Listener's presence . . . into awareness and with that awareness the total situation [will be] altered" in holy and healing ways.

Notes

1. Douglas V. Steere, *On Listening to One Another*, 25, in Susan K. Hedahl, *Listening Ministry: Rethinking Pastoral Leadership* (Minneapolis: Fortress, 2001), 47.

2. Hedahl, *Listening Ministry*, 44.

3. Lawrence E. Holst, ed., *Hospital Ministry: The Role of the Chaplain Today* (New York: Crossroad, 1985), 46, cited in John Quinlan, *Pastoral Relatedness: The Essence of Pastoral Care* (Lanham, MD: University Press of America, 2002), xvi.

4. Paul W. Pruyser, *The Minister as Diagnostician* (Philadelphia: Westminster Press, 1976); the presentation here is based on Pruyser's original work. A more recent interpretation is offered in Howard W. Stone, *Theological Context for Pastoral Caregiving: Word in Deed* (Binghamton, NY: Haworth Pastoral Press, 1996), chapter 3.

5. For a full description of these categories, see Pruyser, *Minister as Diagnostician*, especially chapter 5. The dimensions described here are based on both Pruyser and Stone (see previous footnote), as adapted by the author based on her pastoral experiences.

6. Ernest Jones, in Pruyser, *Minister as Diagnostician*, 64.

7. Stone, *Theological Context for Pastoral Caregiving*, 55.

8. Hyung Kyung Chung, in Paul R. Smith, *Is It Okay to Call God "Mother"?* (Peabody, MA: Hendrickson Publishers, 1993), 21.

Chapter Six

Sacred Words, Sacred Actions

*Ritual is the license we give one another and God to don bright
colors and move in circles and claim this moment as a kairos.
Only where there is death does ritual cease. Without it we
literally die.*[1]

WHETHER YOU KNOW IT or not, you have been participating
in rituals all your life. You have attended and created birth-
day parties. You know how to act at a Little League game, and
how Super Bowl parties work. You've gone to graduations, weddings, and funerals. At the purely social level, all of us are familiar
and comfortable with rituals.

Although their shapes may be different, rituals appear in every
culture.[2] Whatever their form, rituals outline and preserve social
and spiritual order, create and foster community, and feed and
nurture human spirits.

In the varied events of their lives, human beings everywhere
seek forms, words, and actions that mark and respond to those
events, and that remind them of God's presence in their midst.
They find or create the opportunities to "don bright colors and
move in circles and claim [the] moment as kairos" that are called
"rituals."

Ritual Then and Now

Our Scriptural Tradition

Our scriptural tradition reveals the importance of rituals to faithful
people across time. The Old Testament shows us how ancient ones

planted and harvested their crops in certain ways, offered specially prepared meals of hospitality, prepared and offered sacrifices, built altars and places of meeting, anointed and blessed their leaders, and in those acts felt more deeply connected to the Holy.

Jesus continued many of those traditions. He read scripture to worshipers in the Temple and prayed for those seeking God's help. He danced at their weddings, smeared mud on their eyes, cast out their demons, ate at their dinner tables, and broke bread and poured wine and shared them with his followers. Through words and actions, he helped make the Holy real for those he served.

Rituals and Faith Today

While most people are comfortable with social rituals, they may be less so with religious rituals. Depending on your faith tradition, the word "ritual" may even make you a little uneasy. Tom Driver describes his experience growing up in the Methodist tradition in the American South. In his faith community, there was a large divide between what was seen as acceptable religious practice (going to church) and this odd thing called "ritual." For his family, " 'church service' referred to something God-given and true, while 'ritual' was viewed with suspicion as some kind of esoteric activity practiced by people of 'other faiths' — that is … by Anglicans, Roman Catholics, Jews, Muslims, and all manner of pagans."[3]

You may recognize what he is talking about. In much of mainstream Protestantism, "ritual" has gotten a bad name. Most Protestants have come to rely increasingly on linear, logical thought as the way the world (including that of faith) is to be explored and understood. In contrast, rituals, which may suggest a more nonlinear, intuitive way of understanding, have come to connote "primitive" or unsophisticated thinking and doing.

Most faith traditions have developed their own set of rules that define which rituals are acceptable and which are not. Prayer, for example, is considered an acceptable ritual in most faith communities, as are the celebration of Holy Communion and baptism. Beyond those, however, there is considerable argument about what rituals may be considered legitimate faith practices, which can present a problem in pastoral caregiving. Consider the following example.

The Dog Funeral

Some years ago, a colleague of mine was working as a hospice chaplain. She called on James, a man whom she had visited twice before. He was dying and utterly alone, with no family or friends. His hospice caregivers were all he had by way of "family" — except for an ancient dog.

This dog, a scruffy brown terrier, was named Simon. James's one hope was that Simon would go to a good home when James died. But on the morning my colleague went to visit, James had wakened to find Simon lying cold and still on the bed next to him. He was devastated, and he begged her to conduct a funeral for his dog.

She brought this case to her pastoral supervision group because she was worried in hindsight that she had not been very helpful to James. In her denomination, clergy did not do funerals for animals. So she had refused James's request, explaining that it was "against the rules" for her to do a funeral for Simon. A few days later James too had died — and now she was feeling guilty for having denied him something that might have given him some comfort and peace. She wondered whether the passing of his beloved animal companion should have been marked by some kind of ritual whether or not her tradition authorized such observances.

Her quandary is not an unusual one. Many of our churches seem to have lost sight of the imperative human needs met by ritual. The people to whom churches *say* they want to minister live rich, complex lives, filled with events that *need* to be ritually observed. Yet when those times come, either the rules prohibit doing so, or the tradition lacks the resources to provide effective rituals to help caregivers and careseekers.

Parents-to-be lose children-to-be through miscarriages or still-births, and need to be able to mark and grieve those losses. Nontraditional couples choose to join their lives together, and need to celebrate that in community. Couples sever their relationships, and need to mark those endings. People retire from lifelong work, and need to have that transition acknowledged. Lives are filled with beginnings, endings, and in-between joys and sorrows, many of which merit ritual observances as a way of connecting those persons, those events, and God.

In this chapter, we explore how three traditional rituals of the church may be used in helpful ways in pastoral care. We also consider how, when you can't easily find appropriate rituals for use in your caregiving, you may create the rituals that are needed.

Sharing Scripture

What You Need to Know

Before you can use any resource or tool effectively, you need to be familiar with it. Depending on the tradition in which you were raised, you may or may not feel like you have a well-developed knowledge of scripture, its origins, and how it is interpreted. The good news is that the longer you are in ministry, particularly if your ministry includes preaching and teaching, the more familiar you will become with this rich faith foundation and resource. The challenging news is that there is always more to learn. Even if you have read the Bible all your life, regular study — of the text itself, of good Bible commentaries, and of contemporary scholarship — will help you deepen your understanding and appreciation. The more you learn, the more effectively you will be able to use scripture with others.

Therefore, one of your pastoral tasks is to develop a regular study practice of your own. Everyone does it differently, but the key is really working through biblical passages. Read the text — pray the text — then see what commentators have to say. Make

notes in the margins of your Bible. What do you notice? What
stands out for you? With what do you struggle? How? Why? What
passages are helpful to you during your times of spiritual difficulty?
If they are helpful to you, they may also be helpful to others.

A second task is to learn how your tradition understands the
meaning and authority of scripture, and how it is to be used in
pastoral care.[4] For example, do you understand the Bible as the
literal word of God, or as the work of human beings, inspired by
God's Spirit, who did their best to record what they understood
to be God's yearnings for humankind? How do you understand
what it means to "interpret" scripture to others? Knowing these
things will help you use scripture effectively in your ministry.

The Power of Story [5]

Scripture is useful and potent in caregiving because it is above all
about story. Stories, like other rituals, are tremendously powerful. They tell us who we are, and how we fit into our community
and into the world. They help us make sense out of our experiences, especially as we share them, and they connect us with
other persons and with the Holy.

Before offering a scripture passage to careseekers, we need first
to listen to their story — by which I don't mean their "case
history," but rather what is most important to them, what has
influenced them in the past, and what concerns them most now.
How do they fit into their family of origin? What are their family
myths? How has their life developed? What were the easy parts?
The hard parts? What other relationships are important in their
lives? How have those relationships changed over time? What
themes emerge in their life — joy, freedom, abundance, want, despair? What plan do they think God has for them? What life
issues do they struggle with? What are they most joyful about?
Most regretful about? Most afraid of? Most angry at?

If a person has come to you to talk about a specific problem, get as clear as possible about what the problem is. What
exactly is he or she wrestling with? How does this struggle involve

others? What is the person trying to decide or accomplish? What theological issues or scriptural themes are related to the situation?

As always, when reflecting theologically, explore your care-seekers' stories about God. How do they image or understand God? Where do those images come from? How do they fit with the person's current understandings of their experiences in the world? How are they helpful in this particular situation, or hurtful? What other stories might help the person expand their sense of who and what and how God is, in healing and transformative ways?

As you listen, what biblical parallels occur to you? If the person is in pain, what psalms of lament might resonate for them? If she is trying to make a difficult decision, what biblical examples validate her struggle? If he needs strength, what examples of God providing such support might encourage him? If hope needs rekindling, what stories offer such hope?

Once you have clarified the care-receiver's situation and needs, and still before offering any scripture examples of your own, ask the careseeker if a particular Bible story or passage comes to mind for him as he reflects on his circumstances, or a biblical character she especially relates to in her situation. As you raise these questions, remember that many laypeople feel they "don't know the Bible very well." Rather than putting them on the spot, ask your questions in an open-ended way so they feel permission to say, "No, I can't think of any."

If an example is offered, explore how the person understands that story. How does she see this passage as related to her own concerns? What makes the story meaningful to him in understanding his own life, or in struggling with his faith? If a biblical person is named, explore what about that person seems helpful in this situation.

If no favorite Bible story is forthcoming, nor one that fits the circumstances, you may offer your own example. Keep checking in with the caregiver to learn whether and how this resonates with his or her experiences and theological understandings.

Praying with and for Others

The one ritual we are most often called upon to share with care-seekers is prayer. Whatever our ministry, at some point we will be asked to pray with or for those who are struggling, those who are entering or leaving relationships, those who are ill or those who care for them — as well as a surprising variety of other things, including parish potlucks, weather, mission projects, groundbreakings, pets, and more.

This desire for prayer may cause your heart to rise in your throat — because praying "out loud" is something many care-givers are nervous about doing. Even though they may have rich personal prayer lives, praying with others may make them feel uncomfortable, exposed, or inadequate. The good news is that you *do* know how to pray. The growth part involves learning to do it in different settings than you are used to.

What Is Prayer?

Some caregivers worry about praying publicly because somewhere in their faith development they were taught that prayer involves using the right words said the right way with just the right body posture. Your Sunday school teacher may have taught you to fold your hands and bow your head before you prayed, and your min-isters may have sounded especially "holy" when they prayed aloud in their gorgeous resonant voices. You may worry that you don't know how, or won't be able, to do it the same — "right" — way. Yet, says Frederick Buechner:

> We all pray whether we think of it as praying or not. The odd silence we fall into when something very beautiful is happening, or something very good or very bad. The ah-h-h-h! that sometimes floats up out of us as out of a Fourth of July crowd when the skyrocket bursts over the water. The stammer of pain at somebody else's pain. The stammer of joy at somebody else's joy. Whatever words or sounds we use for sighing with over our own lives. These are all prayers

in their way. These are all spoken not just to ourselves but to something even more familiar than ourselves and even more strange than the world.[6]

Other writers help us expand our understandings of prayer even further. The Reverend Jane Vennard writes about embodied prayer, and about work for justice and peace as a form of prayer. Fr. Thomas Keating encourages us to consider practicing contemplative prayer. Thich Nhat Hahn teaches us about walking meditation, Lauren Artress suggests walking the labyrinth as a way to pray, and Gabrielle Roth tells us how to pray by dancing. There are hundreds of ways to pray, each of which connects us (and careseekers) with the Holy.

Framing Prayers

You may still feel nervous as you imagine some caregiving scenarios. You may feel comfortable offering prayer when something wonderful has happened — say, the birth of a much-wanted child, or a patient's receiving good medical news. But what about those hard, distressing times that occur in every ministry? How do you pray when a parishioner tells you her husband has just been diagnosed with Parkinson's disease? Or when a colleague tells you she has just been diagnosed with breast cancer? Or when you are called by the distraught family member of someone who has just died?

As in all other good pastoral care, the first step in framing a helpful prayer is to listen. Listen to the person's concerns, fears, and hopes. What does the careseeker want or need from God? What does he or she need from you, and from the prayer you can offer on his or her behalf?

Listen for whether careseekers want you to pray for them. Just because a woman, for example, is gravely ill, has suffered a serious loss, or is struggling with a hard decision doesn't mean she wants to be prayed for. And even though *you* may want to offer a prayer, you need to know what *she* wants. Simply ask her directly, "Would it be all right for me to pray for you?" and "Is there something in particular you would like me to pray for?" Focus your prayer on her request. If you have trouble praying spontaneously, use a prayer from one of the many good books of worship resources. If you know something about the pastoral situation you are going into, prepare a prayer ahead of time that will address what you think are likely to be important concerns for the careseeker, then modify it as needed based on what actually transpires in your conversation.

Prayer Language and Theology

The language you use when you pray publicly does matter, particularly the language you use about God and God's activity in the world. For example, you may come from a tradition where God is spoken to and about solely in male terms; for example, as "he" or "him" or "Father." You may come from a tradition where God is spoken to and about using gender-inclusive language, or with a variety of images — for example, as "Holy One" or "Creator," or as "she" or "Mother."

Different traditions also have different understandings of how God works in the world. In some, God is seen as all-knowing and controlling everything that happens. In others, God is seen as yearning for the well-being of all humanity, but does not control every event that occurs. In still others, God is seen as managing some events while leaving leeway for human choices.

Be aware of your God language and understandings, and listen carefully for those of the careseeker. Does she see God as shepherd, creator, lover, judge, or something else? Does he refer to God as "he" or as "Heavenly Parent"? Does the careseeker pray to God, to Jesus Christ, or to the Holy Spirit? What assumptions does she have about how God acts in the world (for example, watching, controlling, guiding)? Our most helpful and meaningful prayers reflect and draw on careseekers' images and theology, even if they do not entirely match our own.

But what do we do or say when a careseeker asks us to pray for something that is inconsistent with our understandings of who God is or how God works? For example, that God will cure his mother's dementia, or will bring home an errant spouse.

In these situations, it can be helpful to use "framing" language that lets us honor the person's request by lifting it in a way that also makes room for God to respond how God will. For example, phrases like "If it is possible, Lord, we ask that..." or "We pray, God, that you [do this thing] if it is your will" offer the possibility that what this person wants will happen. At the same time, the prayer has not created a situation where, if what the careseeker want does not occur, it will damage their faith or their trust that God cares about them.

Holy Communion

All mainline Protestant denominations and the Roman Catholic Church share the understanding that the ritual we call Holy Communion — also called the Lord's Supper or the Eucharist — is one of the sacraments of the church.[7] However, different traditions have somewhat different understandings of exactly what this sacrament means, which has bearing on the kind of pastoral care we offer.

In some traditions, the focus is on *memorialization* — on remembering, honoring, and giving thanks for Jesus' sacrifice made on behalf of all humanity. In other traditions, the focus is on *community* aspects of the meal — on how as it is shared persons are called into deeper, more compassionate, and more justice-creating relationships with each other. In still others, the focus is on the *transformation* to which faithful people are called and which they are called to create in the world.

In offering Communion to those for whom you care, know how your tradition understands this Holy meal. What are the primary meanings in your community, and how is this ritual practiced? Who may serve the elements?[8] Is it only the minister or priest who may do so, or may lay servers also be involved? Are special wafers used, or bread baked by a church member, and what does that mean? Do people share a common cup or drink individually? Is the liturgy always the same, or does it vary by liturgical season?

Outside of worship, when and how is Communion shared? Is it regularly taken to the homebound or to those in the hospital? Is it offered only to those who are members of your church (or of your denomination), or may it be offered to others, like family members of parishioners, who also need pastoral care?

Knowing these things helps you to understand what meaning Communion will have for those to whom you offer it — particularly if you are sharing it outside of a worship setting. Depending on your tradition, it may matter very much to the person you are serving whether you have brought bread from the congregation's celebration of the sacrament, or instead are sharing a prepackaged wafer and cup. It will also make a difference what liturgy you use. In some denominations, the same liturgy is always used regardless of circumstances, and those whom you are serving will find this comforting. In others, the liturgy differs depending on the setting in which the sacrament is being shared.

Creating New Rituals

There are many pastoral care occasions for which no formal rituals exist in most denominations, or when suggested rituals (usually prayers) do exist, they may not be the most helpful in a particular circumstance. For example, your denomination's *Book of Worship*[9] may include "prayers for a time of loss," but the kind of grief a person experiences at the loss of a job — and so, the prayers that are most likely to be helpful — is very different from that which comes from the loss of a child, which in turn is different from the loss of a lifelong companion.

Created rituals can be very simple. For example, writing something the careseeker is concerned about on a piece of paper, and then burning the paper, can be powerfully symbolic. As the paper and the emotional burden it carries disappear into smoke, the careseeker will often feel a physical and spiritual sense of release. Rituals can also be elaborate and complex. They might include several people and multiple symbols and actions that connect those persons with the sacred. Practicing Godward listening will help you discern what is needed in a particular situation.

The suggested resources at the end of the book offer rituals you may wish to use or adapt, in addition to those from your tradition. For other situations, you may be able to create rituals to fit particular situations you encounter. Like prayers, a new ritual should be created in consultation with the person who needs it — though sometimes (for example, if a person is very ill or overwhelmed with grief) that won't be possible.

Begin by identifying the *goal or purpose* of the ritual. What kind of connection is this person seeking with the Holy, and why? How might you invite God into what happens, and what is the person hoping for from that sacred participation?

Next, explore with the care-receiver what *symbols or actions* would be meaningful: perhaps light, stones, plants, fire, water, or oils. Light symbolizes the presence of the Divine. Stones, flowers, and herbs offer a connection with Creation. Water symbolizes cleansing, renewal, and healing. Smoke and incense symbolize the movement of the Spirit. Oils have long been a sign of special blessing.

Next, learn *how the care-receiver wants to be involved.* The most helpful rituals typically involve participants in some meaningful way. Embodied rituals — movement, gestures, dance, the handling of sacred things, touch — offer the possibility of deepening the ritual from words said to the sacred made incarnate and allow careseekers to be active participants in their own healing. Together, these elements ensure that the ritual you create will offer the kind of blessing the careseeker most needs.

Summary

Creating and participating in rituals is a fundamental part of being human. Rituals help us connect more deeply with other people and with God. They offer emotional and spiritual comfort, re-assurance, and hope in all the circumstances of life, along with pathways to move between what is and what is yet to be. They help persons build bridges between themselves and the sacred.

In pastoral caregiving, the traditional church rituals of scrip-ture, prayer, and Holy Communion offer great comfort, help, and healing to those who are struggling. Yet sometimes caregivers may also need to create new rituals to acknowledge and bless what is happening, and to create new possibilities for healing and trans-formation. Along with being familiar with the rituals used in their and other traditions, caregivers do well to broaden their knowl-edge of other ritual practices and so to create and "claim [each] moment as kairos."

Notes

1. Mud Flower Collective, *God's Fierce Whimsy* (New York: Pilgrim Press, 1985), 176.

2. Not surprisingly, the meaning of rituals, like so much in pastoral care, is influenced by persons' culture. Especially if you have little experience of working with people from cultures different from your own, you are encouraged to read some of the suggested resources.

3. Tom F. Driver, *The Magic of Ritual: Our Need for Liberating Rights That Transform Our Lives and Our Communities* (San Francisco: HarperSanFrancisco, 1992), 7.

4. Donald Capps, describes three main models for how to use scripture with care-receivers. See Donald Capps, "Bible, Pastoral Use and Interpretation of," in *Dictionary of Pastoral Care and Counseling*, ed. Rodney J. Hunter (Nashville: Abingdon Press, 1990), 82–85. Also see Wimberley, *Using Scripture in Pastoral Counseling*, in the Resources.

5. Most material in this section is adapted from Edward P. Wimberly, *Using Scripture in Pastoral Counseling* (Nashville: Abingdon, 1994), chapter 1.

6. Frederick Buechner, *Wishful Thinking: A Seeker's ABC* (San Francisco: HarperSanFrancisco, 1993), 85–86.

7. A "sacrament" is usually understood to be a ritual practice that Jesus himself initiated or participated in. In most Protestant traditions, there are two

sacraments: baptism and Communion. In a few, and in the Roman Catholic tradition, there are more. You should know what the sacraments are that are recognized in your tradition, since they are a deeply important part of faith practice and may be important elements in offering pastoral care.

8. You need to know under what circumstances you are permitted to serve Communion to others. If you are not an ordained minister, your denomination may or may not authorize you to share Communion with those for whom you care, or your denomination may require that an authorized minister bless the elements first, and then you are permitted to serve them to others. If you are planning on taking Communion to someone who is homebound or in the hospital, you need to know whether this lies within the scope of your ecclesiastical authorization.

9. Nearly every mainline denomination has an official *Book of Worship* that provides resources for leading worship in congregational settings, and resources for offering pastoral care outside of worship. If you don't already have a copy of your denomination's, now is a good time to get a copy and begin getting familiar with it.

Chapter Seven

Are Any among You Sick?

Illness is the night-side of life, a more onerous citizenship. Every-one who is born holds dual citizenship, in the kingdom of the well and in the kingdom of the sick. Although we all prefer to use only the good passport, sooner or later each of us is obliged, at least for a spell, to identify ourselves as citizens of that other place.[1]

I T IS MONDAY MORNING, and Pastor Hernandez is beginning the first day of work at his new church. As he enters the building, ready to collect the key to his office, the church secretary says, "We just got a call that Mrs. Herrera is in St. Stephens. You need to go see her right away." A little surprised at this abrupt beginning to his new ministry, he gathers his Bible, some anointing oil, and heads for his car.

No matter your setting, calls to visit the sick will likely be a frequent part of your ministry. Even if you have experience making such visits, those you make as a pastoral caregiver will be different from those you make as a friend or family member. In this chapter, we consider some settings in which you may be called upon to offer care to those who are ill, and explore some of the characteristics that make such visits distinctly pastoral.

Some Background

Many people are drawn to ministry because they have a gift for heal-ing, or feel a call to become healers. They may be aware of pain in their own lives or of pain experienced by others, especially if some-one they care about has suffered from illness or disability. In either case, they are often aware of the importance of having a caring companion during those sojourns to the "kingdom of the sick."

People of faith may remember the pastoral encouragement in the biblical letter called James when he writes, "Are any among you sick? They should call for the elders of the church and have them pray over them, anointing them with oil in the name of the Lord."[2] Bringing the gift of compassion and the skills we have considered in earlier chapters, you now have the sacred privilege of responding to this biblical invitation.

The Experience of the Patient

If you have ever been a hospital patient, pause for a moment and recall what that was like. What are your most salient sense memories? What did your room, the care unit, or the labs look like? How did they smell and sound? How did you feel physically, emotionally, and spiritually? How did people interact with you? What did they do that was helpful, and what made you feel worse?

Hospitals can be disconcerting, even frightening places. When a person is admitted and receives a wristband identifying him or her as a "patient," that person's status changes. Patients lose much of their ability to make choices. They are faced with the reality of a significant illness, perhaps to the degree that their life is endangered. Patients become depersonalized, a "case" or a set of symptoms, to many who care for them. Patients are treated differently from well people.

As you reflected on your own experiences in hospitals, especially as a patient, what feelings came to mind for you? Common descriptions for many people include the following:

Exposed. When people are well, they take considerable care to protect themselves by the way they dress, speak, and act. They try to avoid being embarrassed or ridiculed by others, or being seen in too personal or revealing a manner. Yet in hospitals, patients are given immodest gowns to wear, and move or are moved around in spaces where total strangers can see their exposed bodies. Other strangers move in and out of patients' rooms at will, sometimes exposing them to people passing in hallways, or initiating medical procedures while visitors (including the minister) may be in the room. In hospital settings, patients' self-esteem and dignity are often compromised; no wonder they feel disrespected and dehumanized.

Powerless. When patients check in, they are required to provide personal information that if asked for by other strangers would feel like a serious invasion of privacy. Then they are given clothing they are required to wear and their personal possessions are removed. They may share a room with a stranger who moans, weeps, throws up, or watches television when the other patient wants only to rest. They are sent for tests they may not understand, and sometimes made to wait days for the results. Meals appear on a schedule that suits the hospital. Procedures are scheduled, then rescheduled for reasons that are unclear. Doctors come and go on their own timetable. In a short time, patients lose any sense of their own autonomy or ability to make choices or decisions.

Isolated. Although surrounded by professional caregivers, patients often find themselves cut off from their usual communities of support. Visits from those whom the patient cares about the most may be restricted to certain hours. Family members may not be able to stay with them due to work or other family responsibilities. Friends may find it awkward to visit, and if a person is hospitalized for a long time, friends may stop visiting altogether. If the patient is seriously ill and in an intensive care unit visits with loved ones may be severely restricted. Not surprisingly, patients often feel alone, and more frightened because of their isolation.

A Burden. Persons who are normally independent and self-sufficient find themselves, when hospitalized, in the position of being dependent on others for needs as basic as getting a meal or going to the toilet. People who are highly competent and responsible, or who normally care for others, often find this especially difficult to accept. They may worry about their spouse, child, or other family member losing time from work to be with them in the hospital, or feel guilty about the burden placed on those family members for doing unaccustomed child- or elder-care. Hospitalization is also very expensive, and those who are sick may worry about the financial burden they are placing on others. Such feelings of guilt, worry, and frustration may manifest as irritability or anger as the one hospitalized interacts with family members, with hospital staff, or with their minister. When this happens, it may strain their relationships with those about whom they care the most.

Threatened. From earliest times, hospitals have been considered places associated with death. Indeed, many people who entered hospitals in decades past did die. Today, however, with greatly improved medical technologies, treatments, and care, most people who are hospitalized recover and go home. Even so, because hospitalization only occurs when a person is seriously ill, they may (rightly) associate being in the hospital with a significant threat to their physical well-being, as well as with potential loss of their livelihood, emotional safety, or significant relationships.

Pastoral Awareness

Being aware that those you visit may be experiencing any, many, or all of these feelings will help you to help them. It will help you hear the frustration under the complaints about the "awful hospital food," and the fear under the shout that "I don't know what's wrong with these nurses; I've pushed this button fifty times, and no one ever comes!" In addition to that awareness, there are several other things you can do to offer the best possible pastoral care in these settings.

Making Hospital Visits

Basic Guidelines

Call Ahead If Possible. A common situation in parish settings is for the minister to receive a phone call from a parishioner saying something like, "I just heard that Sarah Weber is in the hospital.

I know she's not a member of our church, but I know her from our reading club, and I think a visit from you would be good for her." Family members of patients may also call you, sometimes at the patient's request, and sometimes because the family member believes it would be good for the patient to have a visit, even if the patient does not.

It is always a good idea to determine before making a visit whether the *patient* wants to see you. If the situation is not an emergency, call the person and ask directly. If you know that the person is very ill or that the situation is an emergency, you may simply go directly to the hospital, then find out when you get there whether a visit is welcome.

This approach also holds true for hospital chaplains, who may be asked to visit a list of patients on a daily basis. Asking them whether they would like a visit from you, even if visiting them is part of your assigned role, honors their ability to make decisions and restores their sense of power and control.

If You Are Sick. Never make a visit to a hospital or any other institutional setting if you are ill. Patients are already incapacitated; infecting them with your virus or cold can make them worse. Instead of visiting when you are ill, call the person. They will appreciate your concern and thoughtfulness in not exposing them to your illness.

Prepare Yourself. Before going in, take a few minutes in your car or in the hospital chapel to prepare yourself for the visit, particularly if you are feeling anxious. The patient is already apprehensive about her or his well-being; you don't want to add to that with your own anxiety. Center yourself on why you are there, and pray for God's guidance and support in making the visit a helpful one for the person you are there to see.

Identify Yourself. Stop at the main desk and identify yourself by name and church. Confirm the room or unit number for the person you are coming to visit. If you are a chaplain visiting a unit you do not regularly work, stop at the unit desk and identify yourself. If you are visiting someone in intensive care, stop at the

ICU desk. You may be issued a special badge so hospital personnel know you are a legitimate visitor. All of this helps you partner with hospital staff to maintain patient safety and provide good care.

Pay Attention to Signs. Read and obey any signs posted in an institutional setting, including those listing visiting hours. Unless the situation is an emergency, plan your visits during normal visiting hours. Be aware of when meals, baths, and procedures are scheduled so you can avoid disrupting patients' routines. Be aware of visitor restriction signs (for example, "Family Only" or "No Visitors"), and if such a sign is posted on a patient's door, ask at the nurses' station whether you may visit. Likewise, observe all posted procedures such as "Mask and Gown Required" or "Isolation" signs on patients' doors.

"NPO" signs are especially important. NPO means "nothing by mouth" (Latin: *nil per os*). Patients preparing for surgery are not allowed to have food or drink for twelve hours or more beforehand. Patients with other physical conditions may also be on liquid- or food-restricted diets. Do not under any condition give an NPO patient anything to drink or to eat, even Communion.

Closed Doors. If a patient's door is closed when you arrive, knock. Do not simply enter the room or assume the person didn't hear you. They may be undergoing a medical procedure, be on the toilet, or be otherwise unready to have you come in. Entering without their permission is disrespectful and an invasion of their privacy. If no one responds, try knocking again, or check with the nurses' station to see whether your visit is welcome at that time.

Identify Yourself Again. If invited in, remember that the person is likely to be medicated and not fully alert. Also, people who normally wear glasses or hearing aids may not have them on, so they may be unable to recognize you when you come in. It will help them for you to clearly identify who you are by name, and a reminder that you are from their church or are the hospital chaplain. Then ask whether they are feeling up to a short visit. If the person says "no," don't insist or ask them to change their minds, but respectfully accept that they know better than you do what they need at the moment.

Family and Friends. If other visitors are there when you arrive, after identifying yourself to the patient, gracefully excuse yourself and come back another time. It is exhausting for people who are ill to "host" a large group of people, even if one is their pastor. Moreover, with others there, it is unlikely your conversation will move any deeper than social conventions.

Sometimes, family members will ask you to stay, even though they are there. If so, ask the patient whether she or he would like a visit then, or would prefer a return visit later. If you stay, be sure that the patient doesn't get left out of the conversation, or worse, that visitors or you refer to the patient as if he or she wasn't there. The patient should always be the focus of your attention and care.

Where to Sit. Do sit, if possible. Sitting puts you at the same eye level as the patient, which prevents him or her from having to strain to look up at you, and promotes emotional safety. It also communicates that your time there is important. Don't sit on the patient's bed, even if invited. Find a chair, and draw it reasonably close to the bedside, being careful not to hit any equipment, tubes, or bags that may be attached to the patient.

Respecting Their Needs. Sometimes patients will be asleep when you arrive. If so, unless they have left specific instructions otherwise, do not wake them. If they are awake and a staff person comes in while you are visiting and needs to do a procedure (even checking temperature or blood pressure), step out of the room to respect the patient's privacy and dignity. If a meal arrives while you are there, finish your visit immediately and leave. While many patients will ask you to stay and visit while they eat, the reality is that most people (especially when they are ill) cannot manage to eat and talk at the same time, and they need the nutrition more than they need your company.

Keep It Short. People who are sick do not have the energy to engage with visitors for long periods of time. Usually a visit of five to fifteen minutes will be long enough. If they want more time, they will let you know. If, while you are visiting, the patient begins to look tired, uncomfortable, or in obvious pain, quickly wrap up your visit and leave.

Praying Before You Leave. One of the special gifts that ministers offer patients is that of prayer. Before you leave, ask whether the patient would like you to pray for him or her, and respect his or her decision. For those who do request or welcome prayer, you may want to ask if there is anything in particular they would like included in the prayer. Capture the patient's specific concerns that have arisen during your visit, offer realistic hope, and be brief.

Follow Up. If you promise to make a return visit, do so. And, after people leave the hospital, check in and see how they are doing at home. Often after patients are discharged others assume they are well, when in fact they are only beginning the healing process. A continued expression of your concern and care will help them greatly in their recovery.

Caring Conversations

As with any pastoral conversation, follow the patient's conversational lead. What are they concerned about? What do they most need from your visit? They may be far more worried about their family's well-being than their own, or face going home from the hospital with dread and fear rather than anticipation. Learn to listen deeply for their concerns, and to not make assumptions about how they feel or what they require. Be present to their feelings, rather than trying to change them. If they are sad or frightened or angry, let them be that way instead of trying to cheer them up or help them see the "bright side" of things. They may well need your support to weep or to grieve what they have lost. Instead of approaching your visit with a plan for what needs to happen, learn to be open to the possibilities in the moment.

Be sensitive to whether they want to talk about "deep" things or about how the local football team is doing. They may or may not want to talk about their medical situation. They may have ultimate concerns on their minds and hearts, and appreciate the chance to talk to someone who can help them reflect deeply on hard things. On the other hand, they may prefer to forget temporarily about their situation, and talking about everyday community issues or matters of interest may lift their spirits and help them feel connected.

It is *your* job to do the conversational work. Patients are ill, and they do not have the strength nor the obligation to entertain their visitors, including their ministers. Patients should not be put in the position of taking care of you. You are the one responsible for keeping the conversational ball rolling, and for knowing when it is time to end the visit.

Perhaps most important of all, do not give medical advice. It is their doctor's job to diagnose and treat the patient. Don't criticize or question the medical staff's judgment. Don't pass on stories you have heard from other patients about a particular physician. Undermining a patient's confidence in his or her caregivers is extremely unhelpful.

If patients have concerns about the care they are receiving, connect them first with the hospital's (or nursing home's) patient advocate. If there isn't one, or if the patient is still distressed, you may engage — professionally, respectfully, and appropriately — in interceding on their behalf. Ministers are part of the care team, even if they are not officially on the hospital payroll. Whatever transpires, your chief concern, along with that of the medical staff, is the well-being of the patient.

Being Sensitive to Cultural Issues

Different cultures respond to issues of illness, treatment, and hospitalization in different ways. Neville Kirkwood offers a helpful example of this for hospital caregivers. When a chaplain of one ethnic origin visited a family from another culture, he was surprised that the family was showing no apparent signs of grief or talking about the imminent death of their family patriarch. He worried that they weren't grieving "correctly," or that perhaps they didn't understand the severity of the patient's condition.

The reality was that in their culture only certain male relatives were given access to medical information about the patriarch, and they decided what information would be passed on to the remaining family. Further, in their culture it was considered unacceptable to mention the possibility of a terminal condition, because doing so was to open the possibility for its fulfillment. As a result, they were not discussing the impending death in part because most of the family was not aware it was likely to occur, and in part because of cultural prohibitions. If the caregiver had intervened, not knowing these things, his behavior would have been disrespectful and unhelpful.

Persons' cultural backgrounds may also affect their reactions to various medical practices. Their beliefs and customs shape how they respond to basic care procedures like dietary restrictions or toileting modes, as well as to more serious interventions like transfusions, organ or tissue transplants, and autopsies. What may be acceptable to persons from one culture may be met with resistance or outrage by persons from another background.

Remember, if you are ministering to persons from a different culture from your own, try not to make assumptions about how people "should" be feeling or acting. Instead, learn everything you can about how they understand what is happening and how they are feeling about that, so you can offer them the best support possible.

Some Special Situations

Presurgery and Postsurgery Visits

When I was a hospital chaplain, one of my routine duties was making predawn visits to patients scheduled for surgery that day. I sometimes groaned at getting up so early, but I could tell how much most patients appreciated the visits. I didn't really comprehend the depth of this appreciation until I was awaiting a surgery of my own.

Like most patients in this situation, I was terrified of what might happen and worried about the outcome. Unexpectedly, a pastor friend of mine arrived at the hospital at 5:30 a.m. to pray with me before I went into the operating room. His presence and prayer were profoundly reassuring, comforting, and healing to me.

Similarly, your visits to people facing surgery can fill them with the confidence and hope they need to enhance their surgical outcome. Such visits can also be of great help to family members who are fearful about the well-being of their loved one.

Plan to arrive no sooner than twenty to thirty minutes before the person's surgery is scheduled, so that staff will have time to do their preparatory work with the patient. Check in with unit staff when you arrive. If they are still prepping the patient, stay out of the room until they are finished. Knock before entering the room. Follow the patient's lead conversationally. Sometimes they will simply want you to sit quietly with them. Other times, they will welcome the distraction of quiet conversation. Offer to pray with them and with family members if they are there.

After the patient leaves for surgery, if family members request it and you can manage it, it is very helpful to sit with them while they await the surgery's completion. You can encourage them over a cup of coffee and offer whatever spiritual support they need.

Patients often appreciate visits after their surgery as well. While you may want to call and check on the surgical outcome the same day, don't visit until the patient has had a day to begin to recover. Remember that they are likely to be in pain, and keep your visits brief.

Visiting Children

Unfortunately, many parish pastors do not see young people as "real" parishioners, and may not visit them when they are ill, though they need your care just as much as adults do. Yet visiting young people is a little different from visiting adults. It is most helpful to:

- Talk to the children, not down to them, and not to their parents while you are with the child. You can minister to the parents in a separate setting, after your visit with the child or youth.

- Focus on the child's or youth's concerns.

- Don't negate their feelings (for example, "Oh, it's not that bad"), and especially don't tell them they should or should not feel a certain way (for example, "You're not really afraid; you should be happy they can fix your boo-boo").

- Facilitate sharing by offering children paper and crayons, a small toy, or a book. Teenagers prefer visits from other teenagers, so providing transport for the patient's friends to visit is very caring. Whatever kind of interaction you have with the child or youth, it will be your genuinely caring presence that matters the most.

Other Settings

Visiting Shut-Ins

When people become chronically ill or debilitated, they may be confined to their own homes. Unable to get out and about and attend to many of their own basic needs, they often become depressed or angry and isolated. Visits from pastoral caregivers are usually welcomed and healing.

While many of the principles for visiting the sick in hospitals also apply to home visits, several goals are also specific to visitation of shut-ins. The first is to nurture their sense of connection to a community (their faith family) with which they no longer have regular contact.

One way to do this is through sharing Communion. A visit from the minister, perhaps accompanied by a deacon, reminds the homebound person that she or he is still part of the wider church family. Visits from trained laypersons are wonderfully healing. Sharing resources like tapes of recent sermons or worship services or copies of the church newsletter also bolsters persons' feelings of connection.

A second goal for these visits is to nurture a sense of continuing contribution from those at home. This is deeply important, especially if the shut-in has always been an active member of the church. It may take some creativity, but it is often possible to find ways that shut-ins can feel needed and generative. They may be able and willing to make crafts for the annual church fund-raiser, or enjoy serving on the church prayer chain. Finding meaningful tasks for these people to do will help them feel that they still belong to the community that is their faith home.

A third goal is to help shut-ins identify and access resources that help them feel as active and as well as possible. These might include practical items that let them live more comfortably (for example, a microwave or small toaster-oven to make it possible for them to continue to cook for themselves; a special phone set could make telephone conversations easier). Perhaps you could help them access meal delivery programs in the community, find a housekeeper willing to help with home care, or find someone to do lawn care or small repair jobs. You might also help connect careseekers with appropriate support groups, or assist with transportation so they can attend occasional church or social activities. Whatever you can do to encourage the person to stay engaged with life and with other people will be of benefit to them.

Visiting in Nursing Homes

As one author notes, "Visiting in nursing homes is probably the most challenging, the most dreaded, the most rewarding, and the most neglected area of visitation."[3] While most ministers readily make hospital visits and often visit those who are homebound, we may make visits to nursing homes our last priority.

We may reason that nursing home residents are too debilitated cognitively to know who we are. Or that it's hard to think of things to talk about. Or that it's too uncomfortable, because nursing homes often smell bad. Or that it's depressing, since it reminds us that one day we will be old and may be living in a similar institution.

Those things are all possible, yet nursing home visits can be among the most rewarding ones we make, because they are so deeply appreciated by those we visit. Even persons with advanced dementia are aware when a person who genuinely cares about them is there, and we may see a spark in their eye that isn't visible any other time.

Most people living in nursing homes, just like people everywhere else, are delighted to share their stories with a good listener. Our comment about a plant on their windowsill or a card obviously made by a child may be enough to start a conversation that connects us deeply with each other and with God. Sharing a simple treat like a cup of ice cream or a short walk in the garden of the facility can have great meaning and offer deep joy for both parties.

Most principles for making hospital visits apply here too, along with a few special suggestions when visiting in nursing homes. Dress in bright and cheerful colors. Older people may have trouble seeing, and bright colors are more visible and psychologically heartening. Listen carefully to their stories, inviting them to elaborate on details. Remember that their past is a cherished treasure and may be the most important thing they have to offer to you. Play board games or cards if the person enjoys those activities. Join in one of the social activities at the facility, or join the careseeker at a meal, if possible. You may discover you are sharing Communion through a piece of chocolate cake and a cup of tea.

Offer to do something with them, like writing cards or letters. If possible, take them out, perhaps for a short shopping trip or a meal. These excursions can be a great gift, offering them a sense of still belonging to what some residents describe as the "real world."

Finally, never make a promise that you cannot keep. If you promise to bring pictures of your grandchild to share, do it. If you say that you will be there on a certain day at a particular time, be there then. It is heartbreaking for residents who wait for hours for a visitor who never shows up. In our culture, nursing home residents have become the "least of these," so remember Who it is that you are truly visiting and to Whom it is that you are offering care.

Summary

Visiting the sick is a special and vital ministry that takes gifts of commitment, patience, and great compassion. It also offers gifts to the one who visits. You will find your heart growing wider and your ministerial skills growing deeper each time you make such a visit. You may discover depths of courage, endurance, or love that you didn't know you had. Above all, you will meet God in new ways, in the faces and persons of those you visit, as you share together some of the most sacred moments of their lives.

Notes

1. Susan Sontag, *Illness as Metaphor and AIDS and Its Metaphors* (New York: Picador, 2001), 3.

2. James 5:14 NRSV

3. Katie Maxwell, *Bedside Manners: A Practical Guide for Visiting the Ill* (Grand Rapids: Baker Books, 2005), 53.

Chapter Eight

A Time to Weep

As the rain hides the stars, as the autumn mist hides the hills, as the clouds veil the blue of the sky, so the dark happenings of my lot hide the shining of your face from me. Yet, if I may hold your hand in the darkness, it is enough.[1]

CARING FOR THE DYING and those who grieve is especially challenging and demanding. Yet these situations also offer opportunities to perceive and share God's presence in remarkable ways. As others allow you into the most tender places in their lives, you will know you are standing on holy ground, and you will find yourself touched, humbled, and gladdened by unexpected grace. And when you offer pastoral care with wisdom, mercy, and compassion, it helps suffering people remember that God is indeed "holding their hand in the darkness."

The Early Morning Call

We return now to the example with which chapter 3 began — the predawn phone call that tells you one of your parishioners has died, a woman with whom you had long walked through her encounter with cancer. In recent weeks she had grown critically ill, and when you visited two days earlier it was clear she was growing weaker. So while the news of her death does not surprise you, you are deeply saddened, as you admired and liked this woman very much. Despite your sadness, you are glad you have been called to come. And, as a caring pastor, you are also concerned about how you will help her grieving family. In this chapter, you will learn more about how to do that.

Loss and Grief

Loss Happens

While our example is one of very great loss, life is filled with losses of many kinds. Children lose their egocentrism as they move into the school world. Young adults lose friends as they leave home to attend college or begin a job. Older adults lose their confidence in their bodies' healthy functioning. Almost from birth to death, loss is part of life.

Even good losses can lead to stress or uneasiness. Getting married, entering a new educational program, or starting a new job all involve loss, even when those changes are eagerly anticipated. Bad losses — of health, loved ones, financial well-being — are even more difficult.

Although it is a natural part of life, loss invariably causes discomfort, if not outright pain and distress, as people struggle to adjust to a new way of being or living. All losses, even relatively small ones, also involve grief.

Dimensions of Grief

D. K. Switzer defines grief as "the complex interaction of affective, cognitive, physiological, and behavioral responses to the loss by any means of a person, place, thing, activity, status, bodily organ, etc., with whom (or which) a person has identified, or who (or which) has become a significant part of an individual's own self."[2] This definition is helpful because it reminds us of the complexity of grief and its effects on grievers. The characteristics that follow are common, especially in the case of severe loss, but can also occur following other losses.

Affective (emotional) responses are broad and varied. They may include numbness, deep sadness, anxiety, fear, anger, and guilt. The griever may feel deeply lonely or empty, or longing desperately for things to be the way they were before the loss occurred. They may experience a sense of despair, apathy, or hopelessness. These feelings can lead to changes in social function, including avoidance of or withdrawal from other people.

Cognitively, grievers may have trouble remembering things or feel confused. They may feel their thinking has slowed or is foggy. They may have a sense that what has happened is not real. They may feel restless or unable to focus. They may have difficulty initiating tasks or completing them. This may be particularly problematic if they are employed and have difficulty performing their job.

Physically, they may find themselves experiencing extremes — for example, feeling too tired to do anything or overly excited, feeling a need to do too many things. They may sleep poorly, or feel sleepy much of the time. They may have no appetite or be uncharacteristically hungry. They may feel physical distress, including chest pains, abdominal pains, headaches, or nausea. If these symptoms persist, they should check with a physician to make sure there is no underlying organic cause for what is occurring.

Behaviorally, grievers may find themselves losing things or forgetting basic tasks like preparing meals or bathing. They may dream about the loss, at night or during the day. If they have lost a loved one, they may experience that person's presence, seeing the departed, hearing them, or smelling familiar scents associated with them. Grievers may find themselves wandering aimlessly through their home or driving without a destination in mind. They may need to tell and retell the story of the loss, or not want to talk about the loss at all.

Your familiarity with these symptoms will help you assess careseekers' levels of well-being, and will allow you to reassure them that what they are experiencing is normal (assuming it is). A bereaved person who "sees" his lost loved one standing in the living room is appropriately frightened or worried by the experience. A highly competent person who suddenly has difficulty remembering how to make a sandwich or do her job may be deeply distressed by her apparent cognitive decline. It will help these people tremendously to know that such phenomena are normal, and in time will stop occurring.

Grief Reactions

Persons' reactions to loss depend on many factors. A particularly important one is the *nature of the loss.* For example, losing a person to Alzheimer's disease over many years is different from losing someone in an auto accident. Losing someone to a long death from cancer where the person was in great pain is different from losing someone to a sudden heart attack. Losing a spouse or life partner is different from losing a sibling, even one to whom a person is very close. And, as difficult it is, losing even a prized occupation or possession typically causes less grief than losing a cherished person.

The *age at which a person dies* also affects how grief proceeds, with it typically being easier to accept the death of an older person who has lived a long full life than to accept the death of a younger person. That said, it is almost always deeply painful for spouses or partners of many years to lose their life companion.

The *age of the person experiencing the loss* also affects their grieving. Children and adolescents understand death differently and grieve differently than adults, which means they need special kinds of grief support.

Perhaps the most important factor affecting grief is the *survivor's mental and spiritual health and capacity.* Persons who are ordinarily mentally healthy usually manage grief far better than those struggling before their loss with depression, bipolar disorder, or another form of mental illness. People who have strong faith or other communities to support them spiritually also tend to engage in the grief process in healthier ways. Helping connect those who are grieving with appropriate support groups or communities is one of the most vital things you can do as a caregiver.

Unrecognized Grief

In recent years, researchers have begun to explore what is called "unrecognized" or "unsanctioned" grief. This is grief that in the past has not been seen as "legitimate," and therefore grievers have not been offered pastoral (or social) support or care in their suffering.

Gay and lesbian couples, partners or family members of those who have died from AIDS, life partners who are heterosexual but unmarried, those who lose preterm babies, and birth parents who have given up their infants for adoption have often been denied the right to grieve their losses. In addition, the deep grief experienced from traumatic losses like incest, rape, or other assault; from the loss of meaningful work at retirement; from the loss of a partner or spouse through divorce or from a dementing illness often goes unrecognized or unmarked.

Yet persons suffering from these losses grieve just as deeply as those who suffer other, widely recognized kinds of loss, and need just as much pastoral care as do those other grievers. Our faith communities would do well to develop more helpful practices to acknowledge and honor many kinds of loss, and to help survivors move to new places of wholeness and healing.

Complicated Grief

While every grief experience is individual and unique, and there is no "right way" to grieve, normally, over time, people do move through phases of the grief process to a place of resolution and healing. Sometimes, for reasons that are not always clear, this movement does not happen. When the person refuses to grieve, or gets bound up in the grieving process, they may become "stuck" emotionally, cognitively, or behaviorally in ways that are unhealthy and can even be life-threatening. When this happens, we say they are experiencing complicated, delayed, or morbid grief.

A signal that this type of grief may be occurring is when a person who experiences a loss denies it has happened. For example a young adult who has been turned down by the college of her choice might say, "I know they're going to change their minds and let me in after all," or an adult who has lost a cherished job might say, "They're going to realize they were wrong in letting me go and call and offer me my job back." In the case of bereavement, signals may include the griever's continuing to refer to the deceased person in the present tense (confusion about this right after the death is normal), declining to hold a memorial service or funeral, or refusing to visit the cemetery after the interment.

It may become clear that some persons in your care are in no different a place with their grieving six months or a year after the loss than they were immediately after it occurred. You (or a family member or friend) may notice that a griever stays focused on his or her sadness, anger, or depression, without moving toward peaceful resolution. If you believe a person may be experiencing complicated grief, check in and follow up. This kind of grief can lead to clinical anxiety, major depression, or suicide, outcomes that are preventable with appropriate care.

Ultimate Theological Questions

Theodicy

When people are suffering, the primary question they want an answer to is "Why?" Why is this happening? Why do I have cancer? Why does my life companion have dementia? Why has my son lost his job? At root, if they are people of faith, they want to know where God is in what is happening, and whether or why God caused or allowed the terrible thing to happen. The theological term for these kinds of questions — of why suffering occurs and of what God's role in suffering might be — is theodicy.

The prevalent Christian model of God is that God is all-good and all-loving. Many Christians also believe that God is also all-knowing (omniscient) and all-powerful (omnipotent). If so, they often believe that God controls everything that happens. So when bad things happen, people struggle with the tensions between these assumptions.

Here is the problem: If God is all-good and all-loving, why would God permit (or cause) awful things to happen? If God is all-powerful, God could have prevented the accident or life-threatening illness, and since the bad thing did happen, God must have either caused it or let it occur — or is impotent.

If God is both all-good and all-powerful, one way to resolve the problem is to argue that if God does let bad things happen, there must be a good reason for it. You hear this kind of theology expressed when people facing tragedy say things like "God must be trying to teach me something with this."

Your own understandings of God may be different. For example, you may believe that God is all-loving, but not that God controls everything that happens. You may also believe that if human beings have been given free will, then the choices they make determine whether bad things happen, rather than that being determined by God. So, for example, if a person drinks a lot of alcohol and then drives dangerously fast, the accident that occurs is not because God wanted the person to crash, but because that person made a choice that had harmful consequences.

Whose explanation is correct? Different traditions offer different answers. So we all must struggle to make sense of something that may ultimately be unknowable.

Eschatology

If the person's suffering involves issues around dying — either their own death, or that of a loved one — they may also ask, "What is next?" That question raises the theological issue of eschatology.[3]

Historically, Christians have affirmed the belief that human beings have an immortal soul that continues in some way after their life on earth is ended. Most also believe that because Christ died on behalf of humanity and was resurrected, human beings who die will also experience some form of eternal life. Many also affirm that at some unknown point in the future Christ will return, marking the beginning of God's new world order, at which time the dead will be raised again. These all point to the key Christian belief that hope exists even in the face of death.

While most people of faith accept those basic affirmations on principle, when they are facing their own impending death, or that of someone they love, the questions they ask become more focused. They want to know, "Where do I go after I am not here anymore?" or "What happens to my loved one after he or she stops breathing?"

Each faith tradition has particular answers to these questions. Some traditions have definite beliefs about the nature of the afterlife, and many persons in those traditions find those beliefs very comforting. Others, even lifelong church folk, may struggle, wondering what does happen after their earthly lives are ended. Whatever their particular questions, their deep yearning is to know that they (or their loved one) will somehow continue, and that who and what they are will not simply cease to matter when death comes.

Being Faithful

Knowing What You Believe

Faithful people have always struggled with questions of theodicy and eschatology. Their answers have varied, and so will those of persons for whom you provide pastoral care. Be as clear as possible about your own understandings of these crucial issues, and know that you will sometimes be called to work with people whose understandings are different from your own.

Why do *you* believe suffering occurs? How does one make meaning out of suffering? How does it affect your living to know that one day you, and those you love, will also die? At the end of life, what does come next? And where is God in all this?

Persons' most deeply held beliefs often come into question when they experience tragedy or loss. The life long church member who never missed a Bible study class may, in the face of devastation, suddenly find the answers that have long held her or him in good stead to be inadequate.

This can happen to you as well. When faced for the first time with great suffering, the theological answers you thought held true may abruptly come into question. How could God allow the high-school star athlete to be killed by a drunken driver? Why did the young mother of three develop inoperable cancer? What does your faith offer to the man facing the loss of his life partner of fifty-two years? Now is the time to wrestle with these questions, so that when you're faced with careseekers' ultimate questions, you will be prepared to stand solidly in your own theological space, work from it to comfort others, and be better able to respond to their concerns.

Managing Your Own Grief

Even if you have been fortunate in your life and have so far experienced little major loss or grief, as a caregiver you will have to deal with it when it does arise. While good pastoral care includes having good boundaries, you will still come to care about those whose lives touch yours. You will enjoy one person's sense of humor, admire another's courage, learn from another's wisdom, be touched by another's thoughtfulness. And so, when those people are hurt, threatened by serious illness, or die, you too will grieve.

Think ahead: When you are caring for someone who is suffering or have lost someone about whom you care, who will you seek out to help you deal with your grief? Do you have a spiritual director, a colleague, or a ministerial support group with whom you can safely share your pain and receive the comfort and sustenance you need? What spiritual practices might be helpful in your own healing from loss? You, like those you serve, must have support in your grieving if you are to come through it healthy and whole.

Visiting the Dying

People who are dying — and those who love them — long more than anything else for assurance that God does care about them. They yearn for confidence that God will somehow help them through the present terrible situation. And they don't just want but *need* some hope that things will get better. As a pastoral caregiver, you may be the one person who is able to reflect and offer that care, help, and hope.

You do this first by *being there*, and helping them tell and reflect on their story. As you walk alongside them, you show them they are not alone. As a visible sign of God's presence and care, you offer your presence, heart, listening ear, and faith, to help sustain and comfort them as they travel life's darkest valley.

When people have a life-threatening illness, friends (and sometimes family) may stop visiting because of their own pain or feelings of helplessness. If they do visit, they may find it impossible to listen to sufferers' stories and expressions of fear and grief. You may be the only visitor who is able to listen to — and indeed invite — the dying person to talk about his or her feelings and experiences.

Next, as you listen, you can help them *find hope*. You represent the Ultimate Hope, and you can help sufferers find hints of light even in situations that seem bleak. Even those whose lives are ending soon can experience hope in some way. Imagine the fifty-year-old teacher who is diagnosed with advanced prostate cancer. He might first hope to be able to finish teaching the school term. Next he may hope to be released from the hospital to celebrate Christmas with his family. Finally he may hope his death will be pain-free and peaceful. Each hope is real and important to acknowledge and bless.

You can help dying persons and their families find some *sense of control and effectiveness*, even in situations where it feels like everything is out of control. Encourage them to make as many decisions as they are able to. A simple choice like what to prepare or eat for dinner can be significant. Choices about treatment or medications, while difficult, still give the chooser a sense of empowerment.

You can also help dying persons and their families *say good-bye* to one another. Some will welcome your suggesting a specific time and way to do this; others will not. Encouraging careseekers and their loved ones to say "anything else they need to say" will help them deal with unfinished business and perhaps come to a peaceful sense of closure. While difficult, this is almost always a precious and grace-filled time for all participants.

Finally, *never assume* when or how a person is going to die. Neither doctors nor care team members ever know for sure what is going to happen when. Even so, they will sometimes make statements such as, "Well, she's only got a few days (or hours) left, so you had better say your good-byes." The fact is that no one knows when that person will end her time on earth. Your job is to be present with the person (and family) through whatever time there is, and to make it as whole and as holy as possible. When you do, you "create pockets of hope, safe places where pain is softened because love abounds, places where God is invited to fill the void, where sparks of light banish the darkness."[4]

Visiting the Bereaved

When you learn that someone in your care has died, you will experience many feelings: anxiety, sadness, worry, a sense of urgency. Pay attention to these feelings as you listen to the person giving you the news. Take a moment to pray. These practices will help you get grounded and fully present.

Next, get some additional information. Where are the bereaved family members? At home? At the hospital or nursing home? When did their loved one die? Is your presence welcome? If not, don't take it personally; things may be chaotic for them at that moment, with many other people coming and going. Find out when would be a good time for you to come.

If you are invited to come, and the death has just occurred, make sure the family has time to do what they need to do to say their good-byes. If you are at the hospital and the body of the deceased is in a different place from the family, offer to accompany them when they go to make their farewells. Some people will welcome this; others will prefer privacy. Still others may choose not to visit the body again. Whatever they decide, offer to pray with them as they wish.

If you are at their home, and the body of the deceased is still there, offer to pray in a way that includes that person too. Then take the family to some place (perhaps the backyard) where they won't have to watch while the body is taken away. Mortuary personnel typically perform their tasks very sensitively, but you can help them do their job more effectively by giving them clear cues about when the family has said good-bye and is prepared for the body to be removed.

Make plenty of time to simply sit with the survivors, often in silence. This is a deeply sacred time, and you don't need to say or do anything other than be there. Typically, they will talk about what they need to with little prompting on your part. They may simply sit and weep for a while, and your quiet, compassionate presence with them will be very comforting.

Don't try to cheer them up, but follow their lead in the conversation. When they are ready to speak, listen to their stories. Draw them out. Laugh with them when funny memories present themselves. Let them lament as they need to. Learn more about this person who has just died, and about those who are grieving.

Try not to leave a bereaved person alone when you leave them. Remember, grievers are often disoriented and confused, and they may be exhausted as well, especially if the death has been a long time happening. At this time, they need concrete physical and emotional care from others.

Your primary job in these visits is to be present, listen, follow their lead, and stay calm. Your quiet, faithful, loving presence will be more helpful than you can possibly imagine. You will find that families will talk to you years later about how much it meant for you to be there that day.

The Power of Funerals

Although many new ministers fear officiating at funerals,[5] you will learn that these occasions offer opportunities for some of the most powerful and sacred care you will ever give. It is a great privilege to work with people in their time of grief to plan a celebration that both honors the one who has died and helps the grievers in their sorrow.

Your Tradition

The meaning and role of funerals varies between communities, cultures, and faith traditions. If you are ministering in a local community, be familiar with local customs for honoring the dead. If ministering to persons from a culture other than your own, understand the meaning of this service to them. In every situation, be aware of your own tradition's understanding of these events.

In my tradition and community, funerals are understood to be celebrations of the life of the person being remembered, and a joyful recognition that this person is now sharing in Christ's resurrection. At the same time, the service acknowledges the very real loss that has occurred, and helps survivors mourn their loss surrounded by a caring community.

Become familiar with your tradition's mourning and remembrance practices. For example, in some traditions, open-casket funerals are seldom or never held; in others it is expected that families and friends will have time to view the body of the deceased and pay their respects. Some faith groups encourage observances in addition to the funeral, such as evening prayer services in which family and friends may offer reflections on the deceased, or extended visitations prior to the funeral, or lively wakes at the family's home. If so, these are as important in the mourning process as the funeral itself. Observing and honoring such practices will let you create deeply meaningful and helpful services.

Planning the Service — When Do You Start?

Sometimes the family will want to start making funeral plans immediately. You will learn to feel this out, but usually the hours immediately following the death are not a good time to make such preparations. Agree to call later, after they have had some time to think and talk with others; you can begin to make plans then. Usually it takes a little while for the reality of the death to sink in and for family members to get ready emotionally and mentally for what needs to be done next. Don't let your anxiety or need to do something for them rush you into funeral planning too soon.

If at the time of death there is any discussion about the funeral, assure the family that you know exactly what needs to be done. Surprisingly, most grievers assume they need to know how to plan the service, and since few have ever done that, they will be frightened and anxious because they don't know how. Calm reassurance that you have done this before (even if you don't yet have a lot of experience) offers great relief and comfort.

Depending on local traditions and on the bereaved person's circumstances, you may offer to go with him or her to the mortuary to meet with staff and make arrangements. In some areas this is expected, as a way to support the bereaved and to facilitate planning the service. Even when it is not, people who have no local family members will often welcome your presence. Others, however, will see this as a sensitive and private occasion, and may prefer not to have the pastor involved.

A Service-Planning Process

To plan a meaningful service, you need a clear sense of the person who has died. If you knew the deceased before his or her death, this task is easier, but even then there will be much you did not know. Sometimes you will be asked to perform funerals for people you have never met and about whom you know nothing.

Learn more about the survivors, too, including what kinds of relationships they had with the deceased, and what their needs and hopes are for the service. It is helpful, if possible, to have several family members involved in the planning. If, for example, the person who died was a husband, father, and grandfather, the memories and the grief experienced by survivors will be different depending on whether they were the wife, child, or grandchild. On the other hand, the primary survivor may not want other individuals involved in the planning, especially if there is conflict among family members. Even if that is the case, you should still talk with any other significant family members, even if they are far away. It will help them pastorally, and may prevent the conflict from erupting during the service (which can happen).

Invite grievers to share their memories of the person they are mourning as a way to engage with their grief and connect with each other. While not all memories may be happy ones, for most grievers it is important to be able to give voice to whatever their experiences were with the deceased.

Story sharing also provides a sense of the wholeness of their loved one's life instead of focusing solely on their sadness at its end. Sharing stories shows grievers how that person's life, though ended, continues to have meaning. It encourages them to begin to create a new kind of relationship with the one who has gone. Finally, it gives you a clearer sense both of what needs to be emphasized about the deceased in the service, and of the key pastoral needs of those who are grieving.

Next, some specific decisions may need to be made about the service. For example, will there be a casket or urn at the service? Will other meaningful objects (for example, pictures of the deceased, flags for veterans) be displayed? What music will be used? What prayers will be included?

Ask whether the deceased person expressed preferences about what she or he wanted to have happen at the service. If such wishes were shared with you before the deceased's death, discuss those wishes with the family. Personalizing the service to take into account the wishes of the deceased and the needs of the survivors will offer a deeply meaningful form of pastoral care.

After-Care

The loss of a loved one often does not become real until after the funeral is over. Then family members and friends leave to resume their busy lives, and survivors must come to terms with what it means to live a life in which the one who has died is no longer a part.

To the degree possible, you need to *stay in touch* with those who have been bereaved. Even if you don't have time to visit regularly, make brief phone calls or send notes indicating your concern and care. If you don't know exactly what to say, simply saying "I am thinking about you right now" or "Know that I am praying for you" matters deeply when a person is feeling lonely and bereft.

When you can spend time with them, continue to *encourage them to tell their stories.* What memories are most salient for them now? What are they missing the most? How have their lives changed? What are they struggling with? What assistance do they need in their efforts?

Support their efforts to engage or reengage in practical life tasks. A widower of an older generation may never have prepared a meal for himself before; a widow of that same generation may have never had to care for her automobile or manage the household finances. Figuring out how to deal with chores like these restores their sense of power and efficacy. It also helps them understand that more is possible in the future than they may have believed, a sense of possibility that will carry over into other areas as well.

Remembering what you have already learned about the effects of grief, you may wish to *remind them periodically that grief is a process.* It takes time, and there is no set date by which it should be finished. Encourage them to feel and express their feelings, even though they may resist doing so. Journaling, writing letters to the one who is gone, making a memory box, or engaging in rituals like planting a tree or establishing a scholarship in their loved one's memory can be helpful ways to do this. Encourage grievers to be patient with themselves and with others. Help them struggle with the hard reality that when it comes to grief, there are no shortcuts. Truly, the only way out is through.

Make a note of the death date and *be in touch with the family on the anniversary* of the death. If you can, meet with the bereaved and give him or her a chance to talk. It may take a year or more before they are ready to fully process or express their grief. If you can't be with them, send a note.

Encourage them to participate in a support group. Although each loss is unique, people who have been through similar experiences (for example, those who have lost a spouse to cancer, or lost a parent to Alzheimer's disease) can provide levels of empathy and understanding that others cannot. In most communities, hospice organizations offer free grief groups, including specialized groups for children and teens, or for men only. Other organizations also offer support groups to survivors. Know what is available in your community, and help those who are grieving to get connected.

Encourage people to become involved with others again in social activities. While it is normal and helpful for those who grieve to spend some time alone, it is also helpful for them to be with others. This involvement can be difficult, especially if they (or their friends) feel they no longer fit in to their old social circle. However, reading clubs and hobby groups exist in nearly every church and community, and they can be good ways for the person to begin to find new life interests. If grievers who begin to reengage experience feelings of guilt, help them understand that seeking companionship is healthy and life-giving.

Other Crisis Care

If you are serving in a parish setting, and sometimes in health-care settings, you will encounter other situations that raise particularly difficult theological issues and other challenges to offering effective pastoral care. Careseekers will experience the preterm death of much-wanted babies through miscarriage or stillbirth, and will need a very special kind of pastoral care as they grieve their loss. Parishioners will have loved ones diagnosed with dementia, and will need your help in responding to the immediate fears and concerns that such a diagnosis raises, as well as in making long-term plans. Strangers will call the church, or call you at home in the middle of the night, and state their intention to commit suicide within the next hour. Careseekers will be caught up in domestic abuse situations. Church members or patients will struggle with addictions to alcohol or other drugs, which can create both short-term and long-term care needs. Traumas like rape, muggings, sports accidents, and other devastating circumstances will change people's lives forever, and the care you offer them can make a crucial difference in their recovery and healing.

Though it is impossible to be knowledgeable about and ready to deal with each and every kind of trauma or distress that will cross your path, being prepared is important. When actual crises arrive, you won't have time to go to your professional library and find the book you need, or to call a colleague for a quick consultation. Knowing ahead of time some of the concerns that are likely to arise, and some possible ways of responding when they do, will help you offer better care.

Read about different types of pastoral care situations so you know some of the key issues in those situations. Reflect on which scripture readings might be helpful to persons dealing with various difficulties. View popular movies like *Wit* and *Tuesdays with Morrie* that offer profound teachings about loss and death. Spend time with colleagues reflecting theologically on these situations, and begin to discern what theological issues are likely to surface in different situations. Familiarize yourself with resources available in your faith tradition and local community to help those afflicted by different kinds of tragedy or difficulty. The more you have thought about and the better you understand different kinds of human limits and brokenness, the better care you will be able to offer to others when problems arise in their lives.

Summary

Life involves loss; loss leads to grief; grief always includes some degree of pain and distress. While there is no single pattern that grief follows, it is good for pastoral caregivers to be familiar with common symptoms and stages of grief, including ways that grievers are affected emotionally, cognitively, physically, and behaviorally.

Prepare yourself to help those who suffer wrestle with ultimate spiritual questions about theodicy and eschatology. As sufferers try to find meaning in the midst of their pain, you can help them connect in new ways with the resources of their faith and their community, and with God.

Notes

1. Alistair MacLean, trans., from "As the rain hides the stars," in Martin Marty and Micah Marty, *When True Simplicity Is Gained: Finding Spiritual Clarity in a Complex World* (Grand Rapids: Eerdmans, 1998), 63.

2. D. K. Switzer, "Grief and Loss," in *Dictionary of Pastoral Care and Counseling.* ed. Rodney J. Hunter (Nashville: Abingdon, 1990), 472.

3. This term refers to "discourse about the end" or "last things." It can refer to an individual's existence ending, or more broadly, to the end of the present world age.

4. Karyn D. Kedar, *God Whispers* (Woodstock, VT: Jewish Lights Publishing, 2000), 15.

5. The term "funeral" here refers to any kind of commemorative service. It includes funerals (the term usually used when there is a casket and body present at the service) and to memorial services (those in which there is no body present, although there may be an urn of cremains).

Chapter Nine

A Time to Dance

God, teach me to know, and feel, and live the beauty of life.[1]

LIFE IS FULL of beauty and joy, and there is much to be cele-brated. Yet joyful occasions, as much as sad ones, also raise issues for pastoral caregivers for which it helps to be prepared. In this chapter, we consider some of the theological and practical caregiving dimensions in celebrating some of the delightful events in careseekers' lives.

Transitions

Change of any kind can be difficult for people. Times of transition — when individuals are moving from one stage or type of relationship or way of being in their life to another — are particularly stressful. Some of the most important positive transitions in persons' lives, during which pastoral care can be especially beneficial, are those related to joining one's life with that of another person, adding children to one's family, and officially marking those changes in the midst of community. As is true of other major life events, understandings of these events are deeply shaped by persons' cultural backgrounds and individuals' social locations. Sensitivity to the particular issues raised for individuals is as important here as in other dimensions of pastoral care.

Marriage: History and Theology

Marriage is a human institution that has existed in most cultures across time. Historically its functions were mostly practical: It helped ensure community stability, organized and strengthened social order, and provided a structure in which to raise and nurture children. It existed in many forms, including polygamy, polyandry, and group marriage, as well as what has become today's norm, monogamous marriage.

Interestingly, while many think that monogamy was the "biblical model" of marriage, a perusal of the Old Testament shows that many forms of marriage were practiced in ancient Jewish cultures. Nor does the New Testament offer a single norm for the structure or practice of marriage, other than an emphasis on mutuality, unity, and care for and respect toward one's spouse.

Even so, the Christian church has, over the centuries, come to ascribe certain meanings to marriage. Earliest understandings were that marriage is part of the fulfillment of God's plan for creation. Later, it was seen as providing a reflection of God's loving relationship with humanity. Nearly always, it has been understood to constitute a covenant of fidelity, both between the persons involved, and between them and God.[2]

As the church constructed this tradition, it also began to tie the regulation of human reproduction to marital relationships. As cultures became economically more complex, and more people became owners of property, they became more concerned that it pass only to their own heirs. Thus, a set of legal codes was established declaring that legal heirs were only persons born within a marital relationship.

The church constructed theological support for this, affirming the charge in Genesis for human beings to "be fruitful and multiply" and stating that childbearing was a holy duty. What began as a legal issue became incorporated into religious and wider social understandings. Clearly, the way marriage and parenthood are understood today has had a long evolution.

As with other areas of pastoral care, it helps to know your tradition's theological understandings of these events. Learn where
those understandings came from and how they affect those for
whom you care. As you enter into conversation with careseekers
around these issues, you need a grounded theological understanding of these important questions: What does it mean to be
married? To be a good parent? To celebrate those decisions?

Weddings

While our culture advertises weddings as a paramount experience that is always joyful, beautiful, and a perfect expression of
love, ministers know better. The reality is that weddings are often
entered into for complex reasons, sometimes grounded in confusion, occasionally filled with conflict, and nearly always stressful
for most of the participants. Thus, weddings[3] present some of the
most challenging situations for pastoral care.

Prenuptial Work

One such challenge often occurs prior to the wedding itself. Most
pastors require that couples participate in some form of prenuptial
counseling prior to the service. Historically, the purpose of these
meetings was to teach couples about marriage, and to prepare
them for their new relationship in such a way that their marriage
would thrive and endure.

Over time, that purpose has shifted in the direction of helping
couples understand themselves and each other better, so their relationship will be healthy and life-giving. Today the main pastoral
function in prenuptial work is usually that of helping the couple
tell their story and interpreting it with and to them, rather than
teaching them what marriage is all about.

In addition, most pastors try to help couples understand what
it means to ask God's blessing on their pledges to one another,
surrounded by the witness of the community. Finally, prenuptial

pastoral care is a way of offering the ongoing care of the church to these people, should they need it in the future.

However, few couples who come for prenuptial sessions are interested in any of those things. They are usually uninterested in receiving counseling, seldom have any awareness of having problems that require help, and do not come seeking the pastor's advice or guidance about their relationship. They simply want his or her support in crafting an appropriate ceremony to recognize and to make their marriage "official" in some way. The challenge for the pastoral caregiver then is to do whatever is possible to help them reflect at least a little on the meaning and importance of what they are doing, and how it is connected with their spiritual life.

A Possible Process

Every pastor does prenuptial work differently, depending on the understandings and requirements of his or her tradition. Most pastors require two to three meetings with couples, often with the following shape: The first meeting is a time to get acquainted; answer basic questions the couple may have about legalities, church policies, and the like; and perhaps explore briefly why they are interested in getting married in the church, especially if they are not presently involved in a faith community. The second meeting typically focuses on some exploration of the couple's relationship with an eye to its strengths and the kinds of challenges likely to present themselves to this particular couple in the future. The third meeting usually focuses on planning the service itself.

In the first meeting, you may invite them to begin to tell you their story. Ask questions like: How did you meet? How long have you known each other? Have you been living together? How has that been for you so far? What made you decide to get married? What does it mean to you to be married? Why is it meaningful for you to have a church wedding?

Between this meeting and the next, you may want to give them some homework. Worksheets or questionnaires,[4] including genograms, can be most useful in discerning issues in their relationship that bear deeper reflection. Encourage them to complete such assignments independently. Productive conversations often emerge in later meetings when they discover (usually with surprise) that they have been thinking about some important area of their relationship very differently. Pastoral caregiving in this situation involves helping them explore those differences thoughtfully and lovingly, and how they will acknowledge and negotiate differences in ways that will strengthen their relationship.

In your second meeting, you will focus on their homework and on any matters you may have noted in your previous meeting. Asking "So what did you notice as you were working on this?" will often lead to a lively discussion about their process and how that is reflected in their relationship and to conversation about which particular issues are important to each of them. Notice which topics seem to carry the most emotional charge for each of them, then help them discuss those things in a fruitful way. "Hear them into speech" so they can begin to name and hear more about who they are and who this other person is with whom they intend to join their life.

Perhaps because historically ministers often had to give permission for couples to marry, the couple may be concerned that you are "testing" them to see whether you will consent to their marriage. Make it clear from the beginning that that is not the purpose of these meetings. Your goal is to assist, interpret, and nurture, not to judge, permit, or deny.

That said, sometimes you will learn things in these meetings that make you concerned about whether this marriage should occur. For example, in one prenuptial meeting I learned that the groom-to-be often struck his fiancée when they disagreed over money. If such concerns arise, you have an ethical and moral responsibility to share them with the couple. In this case, neither bride nor groom was concerned about this abusive behavior. Depending on their response to your concerns, you may or may not choose to perform the service for them. In this case, I decided I could not ethically or morally perform their wedding.

In the third meeting, you will probably focus on the service itself. Individual churches often have their own specific policies about wedding services. These policies may include which church staff must or may be involved, when the building is available, and so forth. Often churches have a brochure, traditionally called a "customary," which details these policies and any fees for services. Give a copy of this brochure to the couple when they first contact the church, so they can read it and begin to think about their service well in advance of the actual wedding.

It is important for everyone to remember that a wedding is a service of worship. What this means varies by tradition, but it nearly always means that some form of worship order or liturgy will be followed. There will usually be a sermon offered by the celebrant. Vows will be exchanged by the couple, offered before and to God, as well as before the wider community. Certain kinds of music will be considered appropriate, and other kinds will not. Be familiar with your tradition's understanding of the service, and how that guides its shape and movement, so you can share those understandings with the couple and help them (if this is permitted) select music and other enhancements that will make their wedding a beautiful expression of their love and faith.

Including Children

Today pastors often perform marriages in which one or both members of the couple may have children from previous relationships. When that is the case, you will want to discuss with them where those children fit into this new relationship. To their credit, most couples will have already given this some thought and loving attention. If they are living together, their children may already be negotiating their new relationships, just as the adults are learning how to parent each other's children.

If the children are old enough, you may wish to include them in some of the prenuptial work. Children's needs at this critical time are often forgotten or ignored in the rush of joy and excitement the couple has found in each other and in the stresses of the wedding itself.

You may also include the children in the service itself. Help parents write special prayers or blessings for their children to use in the service. If your tradition permits, include children's vows of love and support for their new parents, and parents' vows of care and nurture for their new children. Consider a unity candle liturgy in which children help light the candles, signifying the entry of every person there into the new family circle. All of these offer powerful reminders for children that they are valued and loved by both of their new parents.

Rehearsals

Perhaps the most difficult part of wedding preparation from a pastoral perspective is the wedding rehearsal. In the past, rehearsals were seldom held, because most wedding services were fairly simple. Today, however, with complex family configurations and elaborate service elements, rehearsals are vital.

Your pastoral job is to facilitate communication among everyone gathered, and to try to gracefully disclose the meaning and importance of the event, so that together, participants and family members will be able to provide the couple with a service that truly feels like a blessing.

It helps to request that every person who will be playing any role in the service attend the rehearsal (including all parents). Make it clear what time you expect participants to be at the church, and about how long the rehearsal will take. Explain that if they plan to do any decorating of the church or social hall, that will be done at another time.

Do your best to maintain and share a sense of humor. Most of the people there are anxious, and if you can help relieve that anxiety with your calm, warm, humorous presence, it will be a great service to everyone — and will make the rehearsal go more smoothly. So, for example, I always get the participants organized at the front of the church, then have them practice doing deep knee bends. I explain that if they start feeling tense during the service they should flex their knees, which will help them refocus and prevents fainting. Yes, it's a funny thing to be doing in church, but it does help prevent fainting, and also helps folks relax at the rehearsal.

With experience, you will develop a rehearsal order that lets you keep things moving and accomplishes the goals of the occasion. Until you have some practice, though, you may find it helpful to consult with more experienced clergy about procedures they have found to be time-tested and effective. The better prepared and more centered you can be, the more smoothly things will go.

The Service

Every minister can tell stories of perfectly lovely weddings in which he or she was moved to tears by the beautiful things that happened — stories about grooms who burst into sobs as they looked into the eyes of their future spouses and tried to speak their vows, or about unexpected and joyful reconciliations that happened with parents or with siblings, or about the exquisite grace of the five-year-old girl who looked up at her new father-to-be and said quite spontaneously, "I take you to be my daddy."

Unfortunately, every minister can also tell stories of weddings that went awry in unexpected ways: the groom who showed up with his German shepherd, bow around the dog's neck, and a specially crafted pillow designed so that the dog could serve as the ring bearer... and who went into a towering rage when told that this was not permitted, even though this had been made clear in an earlier meeting. Or the bride who, when asked whether she wished to enter into holy wedlock, paused ominously, and then clearly and firmly said, "I don't think so." After which the presiding clergyman, knowing the social hall was set with groaning tables of food for the reception, and not knowing what else to do at the unexpected turn of events, simply said, "Okay. Let's go eat."

None of this is said to make you more worried about these services than you already are. These stories are designed to let you know that weddings, like every occasion where there is high anxiety and perhaps ambivalence as well, can be unpredictable. Despite the exquisite homily you have written or a rehearsal that went off without a hitch, things can and do happen. Whatever happens, remember why you are there: to join with a community of family and friends to witness and rejoice in God's blessing on the beginnings of this new relationship.

Additions to Families

Just as people marry for a variety of reasons, they also become parents for very diverse reasons. Some choose to have children so they can nurture another human being, others because they want to carry on the family name, others because they want to be better parents than their own parents were to them, and some for still other reasons. Some people will choose and be able to have children from their own bodies. Some will have children through practices like surrogacy. Some will choose to become parents through adoption. Still others will become parents without consciously choosing to do so.

Whatever their reasons, for most people becoming a parent is exciting, frightening, and challenging. Depending on their resources, their experience with children, the commitment of their partner to help bring up the child, and more, the feelings with which parents-to-be face this life-changing event will differ. As a pastoral caregiver, you can offer encouragement and support by providing opportunities for parents and parents-to-be to reflect on their decisions, motivations, hopes, and fears.

Many parents-to-be today do not see this event as related to their faith practice or as a concern of their church. Those who are interested in discussing their pending parenthood with you can be helped to do some Godward listening about this deeply significant event.

As in other areas of pastoral care, you should not make as-sumptions about their[5] feelings about what is happening. If they are excited and joyful, you can celebrate with them. Questions like "So what is it like for you to be pregnant?" "What are you most looking forward to?" and "What is your greatest hope for this child?" all help them name their delight and reflect on why it is meaningful to celebrate this in community.

At the same time, regardless of their happy anticipation, they are likely to also have concerns. Questions like "I'm wondering whether there is anything you're worried about with this pregnancy?" and "What kinds of supports do you have in addition to each other?" will help them identify those concerns, and may provide you with an opportunity to help them connect with needed resources.

If you visit shortly after a new baby is born, encourage the par-ent(s) to begin to tell the child's story. Helpful questions include: "What is your baby's name?" "How did you choose it?" "Were there any surprises for you with this birth?" "What was the most wonderful part of it for you?" "How is this child like you?" "What are you enjoying most about him or her?" "What is your prayer for this new child?" "How will you celebrate this birth right now?"

Finally, parental concerns do not end when the baby is born. There may be complications with the birth, or concerns about the infant's or mother's well-being. There are financial concerns, around hospital costs and as the realities of the future become clear in new ways. If this is a first child, nearly all new parents are worried about their ability to be good parents. Your pastoral support for them and their infant will help smooth and bless their first steps together into their new life as family.

Adoptions

Adoption has become an increasingly common way in this country by which persons become parents. Happily, for both parents and children, it no longer carries the stigma it had only a few years ago. A growing number of agencies are available to help persons adopt children, and a growing number of children who in past years might have been hard to place are now finding loving homes.

There are basically two types of adoption: agency adoptions and independent adoptions, usually monitored and aided by an adoption facilitator, attorney, or physician. Because agencies (especially public ones) are required to adhere to licensing and procedural standards, they provide the greatest assurance of monitoring and oversight, and the least likelihood that adoptions will be fraudulent. Independent adoptions through attorneys also provide some assurance of ethical practice. Independent placements offer the least supervision and oversight, and can cause significant long-term problems for adoptive parents.

Since adoption laws vary by state, prospective parents must become familiar with what types of placements are allowed by their state's laws. It is critical that prospective parents become well-informed both about legalities and about any agency with which they are considering working.

There are a number of considerations facing anyone exploring adoption. Different kinds of adoptions involve different financial costs. There are also emotional and psychological costs, as prospective parents may wrestle with questions about their willingness to adopt a child from a different racial or ethnic background from their own, or a child with special needs. In addition, while guidelines about who is permitted to adopt have expanded significantly, some would-be parents may still face legal restrictions that are difficult or distressing.

Those considering adoption may need special kinds of pastoral care. If they have made the decision to adopt because they are unable to have children biologically, they may need to grieve the loss of that ability. If others question their decision to adopt, they may need support for their choice. They may need assistance in locating informational (and perhaps financial) resources. And if they already have children, they may need aid in preparing those children for their new sibling.

They also face the same parental worries as those who bring children into the world biologically. Their world, too, is going to change. They, too, have hopes and fears. Helpful questions include: "How did you decide to adopt a child?" "What made you decide to adopt this child?" "What are you most excited about with your new daughter or son?" "What are you most concerned about?" "What is your prayer for this child?" "How will you celebrate this new child coming into your family?"

Baptisms

Human beings have long ritually marked the entry of new children into their communities. The Christian church has also formally marked the entry of its new "children," whether infants or adults, with the ceremony called baptism. Its name comes from the Greek word *baptizo*, which means to immerse, dip, or submerge, since water typically plays a role in this ritual.

A Little History

Sprinkling with or immersing in water is a practice that has ancient roots. Water has long been thought to purify that which it touches, so it is not surprising that water is used to symbolize a new kind of cleanness (ritual purification) in many religious traditions.

Baptism was practiced by Jews long before the time of Christ, when Gentile converts were initiated into Judaism. It was also used as part of infant- or child-naming ceremonies much like contemporary christenings.[6] There are several mentions of what appear to be baptisms in the Old Testament, including the metaphor that God will "pour out God's Spirit" on God's followers.

John the Baptist, a Jew, offered a new kind of baptism, described in Luke's Gospel as "a baptism of repentance, for the forgiveness of sins." Jesus, though he was without sin, was baptized by John in the Jordan, an event marked as extraordinarily important by the appearance of all three persons of the Trinity. Because Jesus participated in this ritual, baptism is considered a sacrament in every Christian tradition that observes sacraments.

That said, there is no handbook on baptism in either the Old or the New Testaments, which makes it intriguing that so many arguments have developed over the correct form and meaning of baptism in the two thousand years since Jesus' time. One of the most enduring has been over the validity of infant vs. adult (or "believers") baptism.

Some scholars argue, based on New Testament statements, that "entire households" of persons were baptized, so infants and children must have been included. Others argue that young children in those times were not considered real members of households, and the practice of infant baptism developed much later.

What is known for sure is that prior to the Council of Nicea (325 CE), baptism usually involved a two- to three-year period of instruction in the Christian faith for adults. Following this preparation, these persons were usually baptized on Easter or in the period between Easter and Pentecost. In the seventeen hundred years since, different Christian groups have made different decisions about this issue, with some baptizing persons of all ages, and others baptizing only adults.

Theological Understandings

The key theological meanings of this sacrament depend somewhat on the age at which a particular tradition baptizes people. For both child and adult baptisms, the emphasis in the book of Acts and later in Paul's writings on the bestowal of the Holy Spirit, and the entrance into the Christian community, become central. With adult baptisms, John the Baptist's emphasis on repentance and moral reformation and Paul's emphasis on repentance and forgiveness are more focal. In all cases, the reminder and assurance that the one being baptized is God's child, along with commissioning for ministry and entry into a new way of life, are resonant themes.

All of this invites us to reflect on what it means for the Holy Spirit to be "bestowed" upon a person, and the way in which that is a gift of grace from God. It also bids us to consider what it means to declare formally that a person is "a child of God." What, if anything, does that signify or accomplish that is not already true without the act of baptism? What does it mean for a person of any age to be initiated into Christ, and welcomed into a believing community? Finally, baptism demands that we live a different way than if we were not baptized. What does it mean to us, and to those we serve, to live as a person named and claimed by God, as one baptized in the threefold name of the Holy One?

Pastoral Care

Imagine that your office telephone rings, and a woman on the other end identifies herself as "Karen Smith, daughter of John and Betty Smith, who are in your congregation." She explains that she and her husband have a six-month-old daughter who they'd "like baptized in your church, since Mom and Dad are members there, and I was confirmed in that church." She then asks whether you can baptize the baby two Sundays hence, since "a lot of the family is going to be in town then."

Your response depends on several things. Is baptism understood to be a sacrament in your church, and if so, what are the implications of that? If you practice infant baptism, do you baptize babies whose parents are not members of your church? What is it that you understand parents' responsibilities to be when you baptize their child? What responsibilities does the church take on with respect to that child?

The better you understand the answers to these questions — and the theological reasons for those answers — the more effectively you will be able to help parents prepare for the baptism of their children, or to help adults prepare for their baptisms. Most people, even if they are long-time church members, know very little about the theology of baptism, the vows they will be asked to take, and what the long-term meanings of those vows are. Pastoral care here is to help them understand those things.

If the baptism is to be for an infant or child, talk with the parents about the meaning of the sacrament, and reflect with them on the vows they will be asked to make, as well as on their willingness and ability to fulfill those vows. If the parents do not belong to a church, how will they fulfill a vow, for example, "to help this child be a faithful member of the church of Jesus Christ"? And, if they tell you clearly that they do not intend to carry out such promises, you may decide to have some sort of naming or welcoming service that will welcome their child into the community but will not be a baptism in the real (theological) sense.

If the person to be baptized is an adult, you need to discuss these things: What are the baptismal vows adults are asked to take in your tradition? Does she understand what those mean? What are his intentions about carrying them out? What does baptism mean to this person, and how will it affect her or his life both in and outside of the church?

Once you have established when the baptism will occur (in most traditions, this is a sacrament celebrated in the midst of the gathered faith community during a regular Sunday service), you may consider any optional elements of the service. In my tradition, we have a formal liturgy that is followed, but it may be augmented by other elements, like special prayers and hymns. In my church, when we baptize a baby or a child, after the liturgy is completed I carry the infant (or lead the child) around the sanctuary while the congregation sings a lovely hymn called "Child of Blessing, Child of Promise," and every member there greets the child by name. It can also be meaningful to place a special flower on the altar, or give a small gift (like a Children's Bible) to the family or child, along with the baptismal certificate.

Baptisms carry rich and deep meanings, and are truly an occasion to celebrate new life with joy and reverence. They offer a reminder of how we officially offer God's blessing to others, but equally important, of how our God offers us blessing, among a community of the blessed.

Summary

Some of the biggest transitions in people's lives involve significant changes in their relationships — especially entering into long-term commitments with a life partner and adding children to a family. While these changes may be greatly desired and be occasions of great joy, they can also be times of confused feelings and great stress. Good pastoral care in these situations can help the people involved embrace all that is going on, celebrate it as part of the balance and wholeness of life, and celebrate the blessings involved.

Notes

1. Karyn D. Kedar, *Our Dance with God: Finding Prayer, Perspective, and Meaning in the Stories of Our Lives* (Woodstock, VT: Jewish Lights Publishing, 2004), 11.

2. J. C. Wynn, "Marriage," in *Dictionary of Pastoral Care and Counseling,* ed. Rodney J. Hunter (Nashville: Abingdon, 1990).

3. The terms "wedding" and "marriage" refer here to any formal celebration of entry into a life commitment between two members of a couple.

4. Most faith groups have prepared materials to be used for prenuptial counseling. Learn what your tradition offers and explore materials from others. Over time, you will discover what materials are most helpful in the kind of prenuptial work you do.

5. I have used plural pronouns in this section, since couples are often more interested in talking about these issues with their pastor than are single parents-to-be. The questions and concerns raised here are appropriate regardless of whether you are working with individuals or couples. When working with single parents, you may want to be especially mindful about whether they have adequate resources and support.

6. Some people wonder what the difference is between christenings and baptisms. In ancient times new Christians were given a new name to mark their entry into the Christian church — thus, they were "Christ-ened." Later, christenings involved anointing with oil and laying on of hands, and might or might not accompany baptism. In most traditions today, the anointing and laying on of hands is no longer performed, and the terms "christening" and "baptism" are used interchangeably.

Resources

Chapter 1 / What Makes Care "Pastoral"?

Love in Action

Quinlan, John. *Pastoral Relatedness: The Essence of Pastoral Care*. Lanham, MD: University Press of America, 2002, chapter 2.

Historical Understandings of Pastoral Care

Quinlan, John. *Pastoral Relatedness: The Essence of Pastoral Care*. Lanham, MD: University Press of America, 2002, chapter 2.

Family Systems Theory

Friedman, Edwin H. *Generation to Generation*. New York: Guilford Press, 1985.
Kerr, Michael E., and Murray Bowen. *Family Evaluation*. New York: W. W. Norton, 1998.

Chapter 2 / Being in Right Relationship

Confidentiality vs. Professional Privilege

Stein, Ronald H. *Ethical Issues in Counseling*. Buffalo, NY: Prometheus Books, 1990, chapter 6.

Required Reporting

Kalichman, Seth C. *Mandated Reporting of Suspected Child Abuse: Ethics, Law and Policy*. 2nd ed. Washington, DC: American Psychological Association, 1999.

Safety

Martin, Dan. *Danger-to-Self-or-Others Exception to Confidentiality*. Alexandria, VA: American Counseling Association, 1993.

Pastoral Counseling vs. Pastoral Care

Lebacqz, Karen, and Joseph D. Driskill. *Ethics and Spiritual Care.* Nashville: Abingdon, 2000.

Patton, John. *Pastoral Care: An Essential Guide.* Nashville: Abingdon, 2005, chapter 8.

Sexual Relationships with Care-Receivers

Stein, Ronald H. "Sexual Relations with Clients." In *Ethical Issues in Counseling.* Buffalo, NY: Prometheus Books, 1990. While Stein focuses on counseling contexts, his points are equally relevant to ministerial settings.

Chapter 3 / The Practice of Presence

Anxiety

Lerner, Harriet. *The Dance of Fear.* New York: Harper, 2005.

Prejudices and Biases

Patton, John. *Pastoral Care in Context.* Louisville: Westminster John Knox Press, 1993, esp. chapter 2.

Hooks

Friedman, Edwin H. *Generation to Generation.* New York: Guilford Press, 1985.
Oates, Wayne E. *The Care of Troublesome People.* Herndon, VA: Alban Institute, 1994.

Boundaries

Cloud, Henry, and John Townsend. *Boundaries.* Grand Rapids: Zondervan, 1992.

Prayer

Vennard, Jane E. *Embracing the World.* San Francisco: Jossey-Bass, 2003.
———. *Praying with Body and Soul.* Minneapolis: Augsburg Fortress, 1998.

Codependence

Beattie, Melody. *Codependent No More.* Center City, MN: Hazelden, 2001.

Spiritual Practices

Artress, Laren. *Walking a Sacred Path: Rediscovering the Labyrinth as a Spiritual Practice.* New York: Riverhead, 2006.

Hall, Thelma. *Too Deep for Words: Rediscovering Lectio Divina.* Mahwah, NJ: Paulist Press, 1988.

Hanh, Thich Nhat. *The Long Road Turns to Joy: A Guide to Walking Meditation.* Berkeley, CA: Parallax Press, 2005.

Linn, Dennis, Sheila Fabricant Linn, and Matthew Linn. *Sleeping with Bread: Holding What Gives You Life.* Mahwah, NJ: Paulist Press, 1995.

Progoff, Ira. *At a Journal Workshop.* New York: Tarcher, 1992.

Roth, Gabrielle. *Sweat Your Prayers.* New York: Tarcher, 1998.

Chapter 4 / Hearing Others into Speech

Going Deeper in Pastoral Conversations

Clinebell, Howard. *Basic Types of Pastoral Care and Counseling.* Nashville: Abingdon, 1992, chapter 4.

Doehring, Carrie. *The Practice of Pastoral Care: A Postmodern Approach.* Louisville: Westminster John Knox Press, 2006, 37–41.

Chapter 5 / Godward Listening

Pastoral Assessment

Hodge, David R. *Spiritual Assessment: A Handbook for Helping Professionals.* Botsford, CT: North American Association of Christians in Social Work, 2003.

Fitchett, George. *Assessing Spiritual Needs.* Lima, OH: Academic Renewal Press, 2002.

Speaking to or Speaking For

Stone, Howard W. *Theological Context for Pastoral Caregiving: Word in Deed.* Binghamton, NY: Haworth Pastoral Press, 1996, chapter 3.

Language Matters

Aldredge-Clanton, Jann. *In Whose Image?* New York: Crossroad, 2001.

Duck, Ruth C. *Gender and the Name of God.* Cleveland: Pilgrim Press, 1991.

Smith, Paul R. *Is It Okay to Call God "Mother"?* Peabody, MA: Hendrickson, 1993.

Wren, Brian. *What Language Shall I Borrow?* New York: Crossroad, 1990.

Theological Concepts

Harvey, Van A. *A Handbook of Theological Terms.* New York: Collier, 1964.

McGrath, Alister. *Christian Theology: An Introduction.* Malden, MA: Blackwell Publishing, 2007.

Migliore, Daniel L. *Faith Seeking Understanding: An Introduction to Christian Theology.* Grand Rapids, Eerdmans, 2004.

Helping People Reflect Theologically

Heydahl, Susan K. *Listening Ministry: Rethinking Pastoral Leadership.* Minneapolis: Fortress, 2001.

Stone, Howard W. *Theological Context for Pastoral Caregiving: Word in Deed.* Binghamton, NY: Haworth Pastoral Press, 1996.

Chapter 6 / Sacred Words, Sacred Actions

Sharing Scripture

Wimberley, Edward. *Using Scripture in Pastoral Counseling.* Nashville: Abingdon, 1994.

Types of Prayer

Finley, Kathleen. *Savoring God.* Notre Dame, IN: Ave Maria Press, 2003.

Keating, Thomas. *Invitation to Love: The Way of Christian Contemplation.* New York: Continuum, 1994.

———. *Open Mind, Open Heart: The Contemplative Dimension of the Gospels.* New York: Continuum, 2006.

See also references for chapter 3.

Prayer Language and Theology

Procter-Smith, Marjorie. *Praying with Our Eyes Open.* Nashville: Abingdon, 1995, esp. chaps. 4 and 5.

Creating Rituals

Anderson, Herbert, and Edward Foley. *Mighty Stories, Dangerous Rituals: Weaving Together the Human and the Divine.* San Francisco: Jossey-Bass, 2001.

London, Eileen, and Belinda Recio. *Sacred Rituals: Connecting with Spirit through Labyrinths, Sand Paintings, and Other Traditional Arts.* Gloucester: Fair Winds Press, 2004.

Rathschmidt, Jack, and Gaynell Cronin Bordes. *Rituals for Home and Parish: Healing and Celebrating Our Families.* New York: Paulist Press, 1996.

Ritual and Culture

Black, Kathy. *Worship across Cultures: A Handbook.* Nashville: Abingdon, 1998.

Ikenye, Ndung'u. "Ritual in Cross-cultural Pastoral Care, Counseling, and Psychotherapy." *Journal of Supervision and Training in Ministry* 19 (1998–99): 114–22.

Kwon, Soo-Young. "Homecoming Rituals: Weaving Multicultural Funeral Narratives." *Journal of Pastoral Care and Counseling* 57, no. 4 (2003): 405–14.

Chapter 7 / Are Any among You Sick?

Hospital Visits

Biddle, Perry H. *A Hospital Visitation Manual.* Grand Rapids: Eerdmans, 1994.

Kirkwood, Neville A. *Pastoral Care in Hospitals.* New York: Morehouse, 2005.

Patton, John. *Pastoral Care: An Essential Guide.* Nashville: Abingdon, 2005, chapter 5.

Cultural Issues

Kirkwood, Neville. *A Hospital Handbook on Multiculturalism and Religion.* Harrisburg, PA: Morehouse, 1993.

Visiting Shut-Ins

Maxwell, Katie. *Bedside Manners.* Grand Rapids: BakerBooks, 1990, chapter 3.

Nursing Home Visits

Maxwell, Katie. *Bedside Manners.* Grand Rapids: BakerBooks, 1990, chapter 4.

Chapter 8 / A Time to Weep

Loss and Grief

Baker McCall, Junietta. *Bereavement Counseling: Pastoral Care for Complicated Grieving.* Binghamton, NY: Haworth Pastoral Press, 2004, chaps. 1, 8.

Butler, Sarah A. *Caring Ministry: A Contemplative Approach to Pastoral Care.* New York: Continuum, 1999, chaps. 7, 8.

Kushner, Harold S. *When Bad Things Happen to Good People.* New York: Anchor, 2004.

Lester, Andrew D. *Hope in Pastoral Care and Counseling.* Louisville: Westminster John Knox Press, 1995.

Theological Questions

Baker McCall, Junietta. *Bereavement Counseling: Pastoral Care for Complicated Grieving.* Binghamton, NY: Haworth Pastoral Press, 2004, chapter 4.

Harvey, Van A. *A Handbook of Theological Terms.* New York: Macmillan, 1964.

Stone, Howard Stone. *Theological Context for Pastoral Caregiving: Word in Deed.* Binghamton, NY: Haworth Pastoral Press, 1996, chapter 6.

Being Faithful

Nowicki, Kaaren A. *Spiritual Triage.* Cleveland: Pilgrim Press, 2006.

Visiting Those Who Are Dying or Bereaved

Becvar, Dorothy S. *In the Presence of Grief: Helping Family Members Resolve Death, Dying, and Bereavement Issues.* New York: Guilford Press, 2003.

Butler, Sarah A. *Caring Ministry: A Contemplative Approach to Pastoral Care.* New York: Continuum, 1999, chapter 10.

Purnell, Douglas. *Conversation as Ministry.* Cleveland: Pilgrim Press, 2003, chaps. 18, 19.

Westberg, Granger E. *Good Grief.* Minneapolis: Augsburg Fortress, 2004.

Yoder, Greg. *Companioning the Dying: A Soulful Guide for Counselors and Caregivers.* Fort Collins, CO: Companion Press, 2005.

OTHER CRISIS CARE

Addictions

Patton, John. *Pastoral Care: An Essential Guide.* Nashville: Abingdon, 2005, chapter 6.

Cancer

Girard, Vickie. *There's No Place Like Hope: A Guide to Beating Cancer in Mind-Sized Bites.* Lynnwood, WA: Compendium, 2001.

Dementia

Mace, Nancy C., and Peter V. Rabins. *The 36-Hour Day: A Family Guide to Caring for Persons with Alzheimer's Disease, Related Dementias, and Memory Loss in Later Life.* New York: Wellness Central, 2006.

Suicide

Hewett, John H. "Suicide Prevention." In *Dictionary of Pastoral Care and Counseling,* ed. Rodney J. Hunter, 1235–37. Nashville: Abingdon, 1990.

Pretzel, Paul W. "Suicide (Ethical Issues)," and "Suicide (Pastoral Care)." In *Dictionary of Pastoral Care and Counseling,* ed. Rodney J. Hunter, 1233–35. Nashville: Abingdon, 1990.

Miscarriage/Stillbirths

Rank, Maureen. *Free to Grieve*. Minneapolis: Bethany House, 1985.

Chapter 9 / A Time to Dance

Premarital Work

Purnell, Douglas. *Conversation as Ministry*. Cleveland: Pilgrim Press, 2003, chapter 15.

Weddings

Batts, Sidney F. *The Protestant Wedding Sourcebook*. Louisville: Westminster John Knox Press, 1993.

Marriage and Family Care

Miles, Rebekah L. *The Pastor as Moral Guide*. Minneapolis: Fortress Press, 1999, chapter 4.

Patton, John. *Pastoral Care: An Essential Guide*. Nashville: Abingdon, 2005, chapter 7.

Genograms

McGoldrick, Monica, Randy Gerson, and Sylvia Shellenberger. *Genograms: Assessment and Intervention*. New York: W. W. Norton, 1999.

Additions to Families

Hester, J. Michael. "Parents/Parenthood." In *Dictionary of Pastoral Care and Counseling*, ed. Rodney J. Hunter. Nashville: Abingdon, 1990.

Purnell, Douglas. *Conversation as Ministry*. Cleveland: Pilgrim Press, 2003, chapter 14.

Baptism

Underwood, Ralph L. *Pastoral Care and the Means of Grace*. Minneapolis: Fortress, 1993, chapter 5.

Multicultural Issues

Wimberly, Edward P. *African-American Pastoral Care*. Nashville: Abingdon, 1991, chapter 4.